The Loseley Challenge

THE LOSELEY CHALLENGE

James More-Molyneux OBE DL

Hodder & Stoughton

LONDON SYDNEY AUCKLAND

A CIP catalogue record for this title is available
from the British Library.

ISBN 0 340 63035 3

Typeset by Phoenix Typesetting, Ilkley, West Yorkshire
Printed and bound in Great Britain by
Cox & Wyman Ltd, Reading, Berks.

Hodder and Stoughton Ltd,
A division of Hodder Headline PLC
338 Euston Road
London NW1 3BH

DEDICATION

In deep gratitude,
to all who have helped
in meeting the Loseley Challenge
and those who have guided us
on our Christian journey.

You are too numerous for all to be mentioned by name
in the book;
those omitted are included in this Dedication.

ACKNOWLEDGMENTS

I am deeply indebted to all who have helped in the production of this book. To Sue for remembering, encouraging and never complaining, to Bishop Morris Maddocks for inspiration and encouragement and for his splendidly written but far too kind foreword, to Mike for allowing me more than my share of Nicola, to Stephen Davies, Shirley Corke and Mary Mackey, Senior Archivist of Guildford Muniment Room, for historical research, to the Revd Pat Ashe, Canon Arthur Dodds and Dr John Adair for advice, to Lynn Fellows for help in editing, and, for memory jogging, to Donny Stewardson, Fred Gooch, Daphne Holloway, Colin and Joyce Reeve, Tom and Phyl Reeve and Peter Williams, to Nicola Cheriton-Sutton for typing, retyping and doing everything needed accurately and at great speed, and to Christine West for all her help with research and production.

CONTENTS

FOREWORD

By any standards, Loseley is a special place. It is indeed a fine Elizabethan house in glorious and spacious surroundings, and yet there is more. It has its own atmosphere that enfolds the visitor with a serene peace and warmth. The owner and author of this book explains this by telling you that the monks had the stones (at Waverley Abbey) for the first four hundred years and the family has had them for the last four hundred. The implication is that they were impregnated with the prayers and praises of the monastery. That is true, but humbly he would not tell you that they still receive the same treatment, for he is himself a man of prayer and great faith, in the tradition of his most famous ancestor, St Thomas More.

It is this prayerful faith that shines through the telling of this tale. Whether it is the vision he has for his ancestral home, or the courage he had in founding the two major industries that ensured Loseley's survival, or the care he exercised over all who worked for him – he would say *with* him – or the high standards he set for his products, and total truthfulness and straight dealing in all his business transactions, in each and every case the backcloth to it all is his Christian faith.

This faith becomes ever more overt. It is seen in the installation of the chapel and the prayer pilgrimage by which one ascends the fine staircase (adorned with acorns) to the chapel. But possibly Loseley will one day be known most for the Christian Cancer Help Centre, set up there in conjunction with Dr Chris Jagger and the Reverend Pat Ashe, in association with the Acorn Christian Healing Trust. In all this he has had the fullest support from his wife Sue, and Anne and I have counted it a great privilege to be associated with them in some of these initiatives, which have borne such fruit in so many lives.

Rightly he pays tribute frequently to Sue, his helpmeet and devoted wife, whose total commitment to the house and estate and all its enterprises has been outstanding. The More and More-Molyneux ancestors, who smile down upon them from the Loseley walls, seem to bid them a 'well done' for maintaining the finest standards in upholding the Loseley traditions, which will hopefully be carried on by the next generation of their family.

In a period of history that has known such swift and at times violent changes, the More-Molyneux family of Loseley have faced the changes not only with courage but with a pioneering spirit. They are a beacon of hope that can inspire others. I happen to be one of the others, and feel honoured to have been asked to write this foreword to a book I have enjoyed, and whose author I respect as a personal friend.

Bishop Morris Maddocks
1995

INTRODUCTION

Over the years a number of friends have said: 'People will never believe the state Loseley was in when you came back from the war: it's so different now. You must write a book.' 'I have thought of that,' I would reply, but there were always other priorities. There *were* things I could write about. The challenge of inheriting the Estate in a run-down condition with no money and death duties to pay. Then the formation of the Loseley Co-Partnership in 1950, providing for sharing our profits with all the workers at Loseley, which brought about the transformation in our labour relations.

Not everyone has received a liquidation statement; I tore mine up and that was to lead to a deep spiritual experience and growing awareness of the importance of God in my life. The liquidation statement was in respect of my company, Guildway Ltd, which was later to pioneer in the United Kingdom manufactured timber-frame housing with brick skin. The Loseley Dairy Products story, with our insistence on quality and no additives, was also worth telling. I have some unfashionable ideas about business, particularly that 'people are more important than money'. I believe in teamwork with employees ('members of the firm'), customers, suppliers, professionals and the bank. I was dependent on them and regarded most of them as friends. If I were to write, my Christian journey must receive prominence, including our Christian healing ministry at Loseley.

In spring 1994 I received a letter from Hodder Christian Books suggesting that the Loseley story should be written. Inevitably, like my life, it's a bit of a jumble. I have tried to be open and I hope that I have not hurt anyone in the telling.

CHAPTER 1

LOSELEY THROUGH THE AGES

'Landowning is a partnership not only between those who are living, but between those who are living, those who are dead and those who are to be born.' That statement by Burke is significant and at Loseley we are very aware of this partnership through the generations, and our responsibility for handing it on. Loseley is not just a nice country residence to enjoy and sell if it becomes too large or too expensive to run. Our situation is quite different; we are stewards of Loseley and privileged to have the use of it for our lifetime. That is a big responsibility.

Loseley, three miles south-west of Guildford in Surrey, comprises 1,400 acres of fields and woodland set between the North Downs Hogs Back and the Charterhouse ridge. The House is at the centre of the Estate on a gentle rise. Loseley is mentioned in the Domesday Survey, when it was held by Roger de Montgomery, the Norman baron who commanded the Central division at the Battle of Hastings. The property came into the hands of my family when Sir Christopher More bought the Estate in 1508. The present House had not then been built: Sir Christopher lived in the medieval House situated on what is now the South Lawn. Sir Christopher's sister married Thomas More's father after his first wife died, thus becoming Thomas More's stepmother. Thomas would certainly have visited Loseley in Sir Christopher's day.

Through the ages many great and grand houses have been built by people of wealth, as family homes and as status symbols. Blenheim Palace was built by a grateful nation for the victorious Duke of Marlborough. Loseley was built by Sir Christopher's son, Sir William More, one of Queen Elizabeth's favourite advisers. The Queen expressed the wish to stay with Sir William, regretting that his House 'was not mete for her to tarry at'. Sir William was not a man of great wealth and he must have had considerable misgivings. No doubt he could have found valid excuses, but he took the hint and built a House that was 'mete' to receive the Queen. Motivation is important and I am glad that Loseley was built to serve the Crown. It is often forgotten that privilege brings with it responsibility; no doubt sometimes tinged with ambition, service and duty seem to have been prominent at Loseley, as with many landed families. In this respect Sir William More excelled and he must have been a man of great energy.

Born in 1520, Sir William More inherited Loseley in 1549 and built the House between 1562 and 1568 at a cost of £1,341 8s 2¾d. Sir William kept the accounts in his own hand and I have seen the original, preserved in the Folger Library. Sir William appears to have directed the building of the House himself and he was particularly fortunate in being able to purchase the stone from the ruins of nearby Waverley Abbey, the first and largest of the Cistercian monasteries, sadly destroyed on the orders of Henry VIII at the Dissolution. The stone is over 850 years old and endows Loseley with a deep mellowness: we believe that some of the peace that people feel here is attributable to the Cistercian monks of Waverley Abbey.

Apart from his duties as Member of Parliament and Adviser to the Queen, Sir William More was Deputy Lord Lieutenant of Surrey with responsibility for raising the army in the county, and he was a JP, which in those days was a more onerous duty; in the absence of a police force, JPs were responsible for bringing the accused to trial. Sir William was twice High Sheriff of Surrey and Sussex and he often had to travel to the Sussex coast to deal with smugglers and assist shipwrecked mariners. He was also Vice Admiral of Sussex, Ulnager of the Cloth for the Guildford area, the local quality controller: all cloth sold had to have his stamp of approval.

Both Sir William and his son, Sir George, were heavily involved in the industrial scene in Surrey. They gave approval for the glass furnaces in the Chiddingfold area and actually owned the iron furnaces in Witley and Thursley. They were requested to ensure that the guns being cast at Chiddingfold were restricted to the Queen's service: they must not get into private hands or those of pirates. In 1562 the bailiffs of Kingston-upon-Thames petitioned Sir William to close an iron mill which was consuming vast quantities of timber. Sir William's overriding concern was to stop the timber felling, mainly used for charcoal burning, which was resulting in the destruction of the Surrey woodlands and which eventually led to the end of industry in the area. In 1567, in the midst of building Loseley House, Sir William was appointed Treasurer for Surrey in the National Lottery, under the Queen's direction. The largest win in the Lottery in 1567 appears as £2 0s 10d and several prizes were won of 1s 2d to 5s 10d.

Sir William was also a Verderer of Windsor Forest, which involved dealing with poachers and swan-marking; in those days Windsor Forest bordered the north side of the Loseley Estate at the Hogs Back. He was also responsible for the levies raised as a defence against the impending Spanish Armada.

Many other duties were thrust upon Sir William, including having as a guest under house arrest the Earl of Southampton, a suspected Papist. Sir William handled this delicate situation with sensitivity. Among the instructions had been 'to bring the Earl to conform to Common Prayer'. The Earl asked to be excused from attending Sir William's daily family prayers and his custodian host responded by saying that the Earl would do him a great honour if he would attend – and he did. The two men were devout Christians: one secretly a Catholic, the other Protestant. It is a horrifying thought that 450 years ago in this country, Christians of deep faith were tortured to death by other Christians because they were of a different denomination; but Sir William was a truly great man and a warm personal friendship developed between himself and his Catholic prisoner-guest.

Not many of us would welcome such an imposition, and it lasted for three years. Sir William personally had to accompany the Earl whenever he travelled from Loseley, to ensure that he returned the same day. Restrictions were eased towards the end of the Earl's stay when Sir William was desired by the Council to allow visits to Loseley from the Earl's wife, friends and servants – I do wonder how Lady More reacted to that news!

Among letters still preserved is a plea from the Bishop of Winchester for Sir William to recover his horse, which had been stolen; and there must have been endless requests for help, apart from all the official duties. It is a humbling thought that Sir William got through all his work, including travelling to London, Windsor and the Sussex coast, on a horse. No Jaguar, no helicopter, no telephone, fax or computer – just a quill pen and messengers, helped by a strong constitution, a deep sense of duty and faith in Almighty God.

The building of Loseley House was a great work, and one hopes that it gave Sir William real satisfaction. Queen Elizabeth did come and stay with him in his House on four occasions; she must have appreciated the efforts that her friend had made in building the House for her convenience, but the Queen was a demanding guest. One letter gives instructions for the drive to be strewn with straw to avoid the jolting of the carriage, and that the House should be cleaner than on the last occasion. The Queen brought a considerable retinue with her and Sir William's family and staff were required to move into the medieval house which still stood on the South Lawn. The Queen must have enjoyed eating the carp from the Loseley lake, for after one of her visits the Queen's fishmonger, Henrie Sledd, wrote to Sir William asking to buy some carp from the pond for Her Majesty: 'I will geve your worship xiid a pece one wt another, and for above xv inches xvid a pece . . . I wolde have the greatest and best to serve Her Majestie withall, although I pay the mor for them.' When bestowing his knighthood upon him in 1576, the Queen said that Sir William richly deserved the honour: few would disagree!

Sir William lived to be 80 and appears to have been active right up to the end of his life, when he was succeeded by his son Sir George More, who was also an MP and was created Chancellor of the Order of the Garter by James I. James with his wife, Anne of Denmark, stayed with Sir George at Loseley on two occasions and their portraits hang in the Great Hall. The Royal Danish Coat of Arms of the period is displayed in the North East window. Sir George redecorated the Drawing Room in honour of the King's visit and much of the gold leaf, still in good condition, is believed to be original. The moorhens on the frieze and the ceiling are, of course, a pun on the family name 'More'. The same applies to the Morus, the mulberry tree, also featured on the frieze: *Morus tarde moriens morum cito moriturum* – 'The (family) tree dies slowly, the fruit dies quickly'. During the Second World War the tree did fall but to the relief of my parents it did not die: I was then the last of the male 'fruit' and I also survived.

Sir George became Lieutenant of the Tower of London and twice served as High Sheriff of Surrey and Sussex. He was a JP and, like his father, a much respected the influential man in the county. The poet John Donne became connected with Loseley at this time by secretly marrying Sir George's 17-year-old daughter, Anne. Sir George was known to be short-tempered and understandably was now furious; he determined to have the marriage annulled, to destroy Donne's career, to have him disgraced and cast into prison. Anne could only plead tearfully, but her father would not listen; he was concerned only with punishing the lovers and getting the marriage annulled. This was an age when marriages were often arranged by the parents and it was unthinkable for a daughter, especially one of high birth, to marry without consent.

Sir George wrote to Donne's employer, Sir Thomas Egerton, the Lord Keeper, demanding Donne's dismissal and imprisonment; he then appealed to the High Court for the annulment of the marriage. John Donne wrote to Sir George, via the Earl of Northumberland, that there was only one reason why they had not asked permission: they knew they would not get it. He added: 'I know this letter shall find you full of passion . . .' That was the absolute truth, but it made no impression on Sir George, except possibly to make him even more angry. Donne was sent to Fleet Prison and the Master of Trinity College, Samuel Brooke, who married the couple, was also imprisoned.

After a year, Sir George was eventually persuaded to relent and the couple were reunited. Anne had twelve children in fifteen years, at least two stillborn; the last one dying a week before Anne herself, at the age of 33. John Donne was heartbroken and never remarried. He composed a lovely epitaph for Anne inscribed on her memorial:

To Anne, daughter of George More of Loseley, a woman most choice, most beloved; a wife most dear, most pure; a mother most gentle, most dutiful; carried off by a cruel fever after fifteen years of marriage. Her husband, John Donne, made speechless by grief, sets up this stone to speak, pledges his ashes to hers in a new marriage under God.

Sadly, the church in which she was buried – St Clement Danes – was totally destroyed in the Blitz but we gained permission for a new memorial to Anne, with the epitaph, at the entrance to the crypt. My family and I attended the unveiling at a special Eucharist for Anne and John Donne in 1986.

Donne became a celebrated preacher and was installed as Dean of St Paul's. Widely known for his sensual secular poetry, he became

admired for his spiritual poetry and his passionate preaching;
St Paul's was regularly packed.

> Ask not for whom the bell tolls, it tolls for thee.
> No man is an island . . .

I have always considered these Donne lines to be among the most
significant statements about our individual human condition.

Sir George evidently inherited his father's energy, for in addition
to his many public duties he built a wing on the west of Loseley
House which provided a chapel, riding school, picture gallery and
staff bedrooms. An obituary on Sir George records that 'he was
little of stature but of great abilities . . . an honester man never
lived'. He was certainly a devout Christian, having published in
1597 *A demonstration of God in his workes*.

Sir George's eldest son, Robert, was knighted by James I but died
seven years before his father. Sir Robert's son, Poynings, succeeded
in Loseley in 1632 on the death of Sir George. Poynings was granted
a 'passeport for 3 years to travell into forraine partes' for gaining a
language and bettering his experience. After his travels he soon
became an MP and was created Baronet in 1642. Poynings had
the misfortune to be on the political scene during the period of
the Civil War. He was in an invidious position, having received
favours from the King, whom he supported, but also being himself
a Member of Parliament. It is recorded that Sir Poynings opposed
the execution of the King. He spent much of his time in London
and there was considerable trouble at Loseley over poaching by
soldiers, who also drained the lake in order to steal the carp.

Sir Poynings was succeeded by his son Sir William More, the
second and last Baronet, in the reign of Charles II. Sir William
was High Sheriff of Surrey and Sussex and died in 1684. He
was succeeded by his father's brother, the Reverend Nicholas
More, whose daughter Margaret followed and married Sir Thomas
Molyneux of Sefton; their son was given the Christian name of
More. It is this son, Sir More Molyneux and his wife Cassandra,
whose family picture, including eight of their children, takes up
a large portion of the West wall of the Great Hall at Loseley. It
was painted by Somers in 1739.

Colonel Thomas More-Molyneux, son of Sir More and Cassandra, inherited on his father's death in 1760. He was a keen and

successful soldier and an active MP who wrote a book on military strategy. Unfortunately Thomas had rather expensive tastes and Loseley House suffered through lack of proper maintenance. On Thomas's death in 1776 his sister Jane inherited; fortunately she was a very competent lady, dedicated to Loseley, and instituted strict financial control. Her meticulous accounts and instructions for housekeeping are still preserved. With a gradual improvement in the financial situation Jane records that in 1789 she was able to buy a carpet for the parlour and, much more important, in 1795 the House was re-roofed at a cost of £422 9s 6d: the cost produced some savings, for Jane recorded that she no longer had to purchase buckets to catch the drips (as we had to do in the 1940s!). When the window tax was increased in 1785, Jane blocked ten and paid £12 15s for the remaining 126. The household, including nine servants, used 5½lbs of soap weekly for washing and cleaning and laundry, 62 gallons of ale and two large hogsheads of small beer a month, the latter brewed at Loseley. There was no extravagance: at Christmas 1779 only half the mince pies were made before Christmas Day, because plums were so expensive that they waited until after Christmas Day 'thinking the price might fall'. One cow was hired and brought up to the House for milking. Jane died in 1802, and during her twenty-six years of ownership the financial situation improved.

Unfortunately, due to the previous neglect of maintenance and lack of funds, the wing built by Sir George was in such bad repair that demolition became the only option and this was carried out in 1820 by James More-Molyneux, son of Colonel Thomas, and who succeeded his aunt Jane in 1802. James recorded that he considered the demolition to be the best thing he ever did for Loseley. Each generation has to do its best in the prevailing circumstances. There was not too much hardship in losing the indoor riding school and no doubt many of the pictures in the gallery were sold and others found a place on the walls of the main House. It was sad losing the Chapel but the family had close connection with St Nicholas Church, Compton, of which they were Patron, and also with St Nicholas Church, Guildford, which contains the family Burial Chapel. Even before the Loseley Chapel had been built, Sir William had held daily prayers in the House. Prayer does not require a consecrated building.

The loss of staff bedrooms did pose a problem: staff were essential for there was no heating except fires which had to be lit and tended, and the grates cleaned, and there was no piped water or sanitation. The solution was found by forming small staff bedrooms in the Long Gallery which occupied the top floor of the House. Things have moved full circle – we now have no resident staff, so the room divisions on the top floor have been demolished: we have a Long Gallery again and we also have a Chapel on the top floor.

James's son, also named James, inherited on his father's death in 1823. He was very active in public service and served as a JP and Deputy Lieutenant and was High Sheriff in 1867. He was also Fellow of Society of Arts and a founder member of the Surrey Archeological Society. James and his wife Caroline had two sons, William More-Molyneux JP, who never married, and Admiral Sir Robert More-Molyneux GCB, who had a distinguished career and commanded HMS *Invincible IV* at the bombardment of Alexandria in 1882. James gave the land for the building of Farncombe Church, School and School House. The church is flourishing today and, commendably, in use for Roman Catholic services as well as Anglican. He also built Littleton School in 1843, holding services there on Sundays; and Loseley South Lodge, designed by Henry Woodger, the well-known church architect. There was still some pressure on finances and the Manors of Catteshall and Godalming, and Westbury Manor, Compton were sold.

William More-Molyneux JP, James's elder son, inherited in 1874. The Victorians were great builders and William certainly made his contribution; in 1877, just fifty-seven years after his grandfather had pulled down Sir George's wing, he built a Nursery Wing on the south side of the House. I am grateful to William for this wing, where I spent the first years of my life, because it has enabled succeeding generations to live alongside one another, semi-detached at Loseley. It is strange that William, who never married, should have built a Nursery at the age of 42. A possible clue is provided by a ghost. My wife did not believe in ghosts until one summer evening, not long after we were married, when she was at the basin in the bathroom of the Nursery Wing, at that period our home. She became aware of someone coming along the passage, turned round and saw a little elderly lady with dark hair, in a grey skirt down to her ankles; she was smiling. My wife had no idea who the lady was but saw her very clearly. Not many weeks later, when clearing an attic room, she found her picture and hung it in the passage where the lady had appeared. We still did not know her identity. The following year, our friend Sir Claud Hagart Alexander of Ballochmyle, a Scottish landowner, came to stay with us. 'I see you have a picture of great-great grandmother Eliza by the bathroom: we have a full-sized portrait of her in our bedroom.' When we stayed with Claud and Etain at their home at Mauchline, Sue was able to confirm that it was Eliza she had seen. Eliza lived at nearby Eastbury Manor, Compton. She would have been a contemporary of William and it is probable that he had taken her round it with pride – or with hope? We shall never know, but she was smiling and happy when she called on us that evening. Eliza has not been seen again but we shall be meeting Claud later, for he is a brilliant engineer and left his mark both at Loseley and in our factory.

William also added a number of useful outbuildings and cottages on the Estate. When the county council took over education and erected a new school in Littleton Village, William converted the Dame School, built by his father, into a church, now dedicated to St Francis. The glorious window in the East end has the inscription 'To the glory of God in memory of William More-Molyneux who dedicated this building for the worship of God on the Loseley Estate.' In the 1950s the then Bishop of Guildford suggested 'Close it down, close it down.' True, we only had a handful of worshippers in the congregation in those days but I knew that there would be a revival.

William was a Clerk of the House of Commons and a JP. He was a keen gardener and the clump of palm trees in the Garden are among his plantings. He was active in the county and was founder-chairman of Artington Parish Council in 1894. William let the House for some years and resided at St Catherine's House, then owned by the Estate.

William died in 1907 and was succeeded by Gwendoline, the only child of William's younger brother, Admiral Sir Robert More-Molyneux GCB, who died in 1904. She had been previously married and had a daughter, Christobel, and in 1919 she married Brigadier General Frank Longbourne, who later took the name More-Molyneux-Longbourne. I was the only child of the marriage. Both my parents served on Guildford RDC and my mother had served on Artington Parish Council. My father served on Compton Parish Council and was a Churchwarden of St Nicholas, Compton. He was also President of the Guildford Scouts and involved in a number of charities, and was both a Visiting Commissioner and District Commissioner of the Pony Club, and did a great deal to encourage young people to ride and to love animals. He was an outstanding horseman, loving all animals, particularly horses and dogs. In the First World War he had been mentioned in Dispatches thirteen times, believed to be a record, and was awarded the DSO, later being appointed CMG. An expert and judge of cattle, he built up the Loseley Jersey Herd and served as President of the Jersey Cattle Society and was a founder-member of the National TT Milk Producers Association. In 1923 my father started production of cream and butter as well as farm-bottled milk, and established a milk round, which in the Depression of the late 1920s and early 1930s remained profitable. He was a progressive farmer on the 180-acre Home Farm, his main interest being in the Jersey cattle, second only to his horses and dogs.

My father had brought back with him from the First World War four of his ex-soldiers. Three now worked on the Estate and George Neville, his batman, became butler at Loseley. There were six indoor staff in the House before 1939 and the Second World War – butler, cook, kitchen maid and three housemaids. The Garden was run by Churchill, the head gardener and three under-gardeners tending the herbaceous borders, the rose garden, fruit trees, vegetables, carnation house, orchid house, vinery and greenhouses. My father did most of the pruning of his roses and fruit trees, in which he took a great interest. He also grew excellent gooseberries on the espalier system and was a keen small-scale grower of carnations and peaches under glass.

My parents never went on holidays because they did not consider themselves to be working – though in fact they were seldom idle. They did occasionally go on visits to friends, but for only short periods, as my father hated leaving Loseley and his beloved horses and dogs.

Hunting and shooting were two important activities on most large country estates and Loseley was no exception. The shooting was let before the Second World War to the Ambassadors' Syndicate. My father had a gun in the Shoot, though he said that he enjoyed the dog work more than the shooting. He ran the Shoot with two keepers, Shrubb and Churchill, and about two thousand pheasants were reared each year and put out in the woods. In the syndicate were the Brazilian, Belgian, Portugese and Polish Ambassadors and two or three high-ranking personages. Not being financially well off there was no lavish entertaining at Loseley in my parents' day, but they did have a house party for Ascot week.

My half-sister Christobel was eleven years older than me so we did not see much of each other; Chris had quite a reputation on the social scene and her photograph had appeared on the front page of *Country Life* and other glossies: she was always 'gadding about', spending much of her time in London. Apart from age, we were very different in outlook. Chris considered the countryside dull and she hated the 'discomfort' of Loseley, especially in winter. It was a cold house, with diamond pane windows, high ceilings, an antiquated heating system and no electricity. Dislike of the cold was understandable, but I could not understand how anyone could dislike Loseley: to me it meant so much.

This era came to a close when England declared war on Germany on 3rd September 1939. During the war, apart from Home Guard and other duties, my father directed operations on the farm and Estate, looked after his many horses, rode daily and exercised the Labradors, inspected and prodded field drains in winter, did a weekly vegetable round in London, sometimes with tandem horse equipage – exciting during bombing raids! My father included among his many friends postmen, porters and lorry drivers. He delighted in giving presents of eggs and other commodities in short supply, fishing these offerings out of his old jacket pocket. Surprisingly, the eggs were nearly always unbroken!

In 1968, to celebrate Loseley's 400th birthday, we had an evening's excursion back to an earlier era, with an Elizabethan Banquet attended by 140 guests in the Great Hall, most of them in Elizabethan costume. We researched the etiquette and detail with the help of Mrs Philipa Glanville of the London Museum, the drink was researched by our friend, wine merchant John Charlton and the food by our friend and caterer Miss Jean Alexander. Rushes on the floor, candlelight, serving wenches, mead drunk from earthenware possets and claret from tygges. Elizabethan Grace was said by the Bishop of Guildford.

The menu consisted of: First Remove – Vegetable Soup. Second Remove – Cold Salmon with Cucumber. Third Remove – Boars Head, Pate, Salamagrundy, Royal Salad. Fourth remove – Roast Sirloin of Beef, Champ Potatoes, Spinach, Artichoke Herts. Fifth Remove – Syllabub, Marchpane.

We wanted to invite as many relatives and friends from the past as we could, so we had a second, smaller Banquet two weeks later. We were delighted that Christobel was able to come from France where she was living in a lovely chateau with her second husband, the Hon. Neville Berry. A number of Loseley staff, past and present, were among the company including my old Nanny, dressed as her Elizabethan counterpart, Farm Manager Tom Haslett as steward, and herdsman Tony Hart as peasant. Paul Getty was also present, as himself. Sir Richard Weston, the builder of Paul's Sutton Place, had been a close friend of Sir William More.

The health of the family was proposed by Sir Claud Hagart-Alexander, who reminded us that Queen Elizabeth, in flirtatious mood, had once remarked that if Sir William had been a bit younger things might have been very different between them. Claud then added his ingenious theory: had that been so, James might now have been King of England! But then I could not have been at Loseley.

We all felt the wonderful atmosphere that evening. The scene in the Great Hall was stunning in the candlelight; music and song came from minstrels in the Gallery. The House was enjoying its birthday evening. The Elizabethan costumes were so decorative, the rich colours of the velvet tunics and breeches contrasting with the few dinner jackets and black ties. The food was ample and delicious. The mead, honey-based and known as the honeymoon drink, was deceptively alcoholic.

Yes, life in Elizabethan times was good – if you were wealthy, if you were on the right side of the right religious denomination and if you escaped the rack and the axe and if you did not have appendicitis or toothache, or married without father's consent. We have much to be thankful for in our age.

When I inherited on the death of my mother in 1946, Loseley was very different from the sparkling house whose birthday we were celebrating on that evening in 1968.

CHAPTER 2

THE INHERITANCE

'Bump!' I had entered the passenger door of the van in the dark and sat down, but the seat was not there and I landed on the floor. The spot that I found myself occupying was normally reserved for a bin for fish offal, to be steamed up for pig feed; the bin had been removed in my honour. It was a dark December evening in 1945; my father, having completed his small milk round, was collecting me off the train at Guildford, returning after four years' military service in the Middle East and Italy.

My landing on the floor was a foretaste of what was to follow. While overseas I carried in my wallet a photograph of the sanctuary of ancient Compton Church: timeless peace, holiness. In my mind I carried an idyllic picture of Loseley, the mellowness of the House with its surrounding mown lawns, cows grazing the fields, the well-kept garden and grounds, the panelled rooms, the well-polished period furniture. All in good order. Beauty and peace.

The picture now was very different. Five years without staff, windows shattered by bombs, no heating, dust and cobwebs covering the well-polished furniture of my memories: war had taken its toll.

My mother's health had seriously deteriorated: her memory was very poor and clearly she was not capable of looking after the House. There was no House staff except for a weird Hungarian called Helen. Helen, in her late 30s was squat, slit-eyed and self-willed. She had little respect for anyone but in the absence of any other help was strangely indispensable and did the cooking, helped with feeding animals and a variety of other chores. Helen kept jackdaws and broody hens in the kitchen and had strange habits, like hiding behind the curtains. On one occasion Helen served up the dogs' dinner for our meal with the triumphant comment: 'The dogs have eaten yours!' Helen's departure from

Loseley was to be sudden and dramatic, but that was a few years away.

Each generation of the family is called upon to serve Loseley in its own particular way. One builds, another pulls down; some make money, others spend. My parents' role during those very difficult and uncomfortable war years was probably the hardest. Electricity had not yet been laid on, there was no heating, as the boilers were out of commission, so there was also no piped hot water: if you wanted a bath you put the kettle on the kitchen stove and carried it up to the bathroom.

The house was always extremely cold in winter, with vast areas of windows, the wind whistling through the leaded diamond panes. I remember particularly the scullery: washing up there in the bitter cold was a nightmare. That winter of 1945–46 was very cold, particularly to me after four years in the Middle East.

Loseley is a large and rambling house with long passages and stairs: not easy or convenient to live in. Many friends had urged mother and father to move out of that cold, uncomfortable house and to live in one of the smaller houses on the Estate where they would have had electricity, heating and a comfortable existence. My father refused to consider it: he knew, he told me later, that if they had moved out Loseley would not have survived. He was undoubtedly right. Unless the buckets were emptied when the rain poured in through the roof, wet rot and dry rot would have set in and rapidly spread.

When calling on someone in a warm little house, how I envied them! I sometimes suspected that Helen hoped to burn down the House 'accidentally'. She would run from room to room with a pan full of red embers and then draw the fire by putting newspapers across the front; they usually caught fire and sometimes fell in flames on the carpet. With my mother unable to cope, my father in his advancing years had to keep the House going, as well as running the Farm and Estate. It was understandable that with no money and virtually no staff things were not in good order.

The Garden had been without permanent staff all the time that I had been away but Neville and Churchill, respectively pre-war butler and assistant gamekeeper, had grown some vegetables and tried to keep things going as best they could. The Loseley garden has always been organic and weeds a problem. Very few people came to Loseley during and just after the war: the drive was badly rutted and pot-holed and there were usually branches across it near the House to keep in the horses or whatever animals happened to be grazing the unmown lawns.

I cannot emphasise sufficiently the debt that I owe, and that Loseley owes, to my parents for staying in the House during that desperately uncomfortable period of the war and, despite their need of money, refusing to sell any land or contents of the House. That supreme unselfishness strengthened my resolve to ensure that Loseley should survive and be worthy of them.

On my first morning back on leave at Loseley I walked round the grounds to familiarise myself. In the Stable Yard I was aware of weeds in profusion in the cobbles, and there were slipped tiles and broken gutters, missing down pipes . . . then old Shrubb, the head keeper, came through the archway. Shrubb was a great character, very erect, very upright, tall with a grey moustache. Efficient, respected, utterly reliable. In the army he would have made a perfect Regimental Sergeant Major. 'I'm just finding my way around again, Shrubb.' 'You won't find many improvements around here, sir.' Nearly forty years later I can remember those words so distinctly and the grave tone in which they were intonated. I went on the defensive: 'Difficult times for everyone.' Shrubb would never criticise his employer, but staff such as he feel a close identity with their Estate and it must have hurt him to see things in a dilapidated condition.

The Farm buildings all seemed to need repair and a number of roofs were sagging badly and leaking; some buildings were in danger of collapse. I found it of no help to try and think through the situation. Everything seemed to need attention, yet there was no money and I was not trained in farming or estate management. 'Change and decay in all around I see.' The words of the hymn rang in my ears and none of the change was for the better. I remember one dark evening going out onto the lawn, walking round in circles saying to myself: 'What *can* I do?' Yes, it was my duty to save Loseley but how? Where to start? Perhaps I would end up in a mental hospital. If at times I felt that Helen's idea of burning down the House might have been the answer, it would have been understandable, although nowadays one's greatest concern is that the House should never be destroyed by fire. I could never have dreamed that we would one day see Loseley restored to its former glory, visited and enjoyed by thousands of people every year.

My mother died in February 1946, a few days after I returned to the Middle East and I got a compassionate posting to the Guildford area pending demobilisation in April 1946. Before the end of my leave the negative thoughts had subsided, smothered by the challenge of survival, of restoring Loseley to profit. After demob I soon began to get a grip on things as evidenced by my notebook dated July 1946, headed 'Planning'. Details include building and contracting, conversion of own timber, lathe turning, canning tomato ketchup etc, lavender growing and processing, horse chestnut meal processing. *Marketing* – advertising. Retail own milk. Shop and milk bar. Canning. Drying apples. Potatoes – get contract and dig earlies early. *Forestry* – planting programme, trainees, portable saw for logs, charcoal, saw benches re-bedded, steam engine for rack bench. *Estate* – list of all properties showing repairs, building programme. *Farm* – removal of dead trees, bushes, brambles, drainage plan for fields (scheme completed with grant aid 1947). Gates and posts, paint all buildings and machinery. Eradicate weeds. Roadways. There were several detailed improvements for the cows, including 'more food – how? more fields? grazing corn in spring, rye grass as catch crop'. *Office* – calving chart, cropping programme, field manuring and cropping sheet, costings, timesheets, milk graph, cow feeding charts, bull progeny list.

I made progress in my first three months, even if much of it was only in my head; but we had to generate more income. We expanded the existing enterprises of Jersey cows, milk rounds and market garden. We added pigs and poultry and gradually increased the farming acreage. Everything had to earn its keep, and the moat became the irrigation reservoir for the garden, the cellars the sprouting house for the potatoes.

Soon after my return home, the telephone rang when I was showing round some friends. In those days the telephone seldom rang and, as I went to answer it, I knew that this was to be a significant call; it was, in fact, to change my life. Donny Bellinger, whom I had met in Oxford early in the war when she was on secret war work and my regiment was stationed in the area, was one of the nicest girls I had ever met: fair, sensitive, natural, full of energy and with a sense of humour. I was excessively shy in those days and I met Donny through Dick Able, an officer in my squadron who generously allowed me to join in for threesome dinners at the Mitre Hotel, Oxford. During my time overseas we occasionally corresponded and Donny was now ringing to say that her father had died and that she, her mother and sister were looking for somewhere to live. She came to stay for a weekend with my father and me and eventually it was arranged that Donny, sister Susan and their mother would move into the Loseley Nursery Wing which was now empty. Transformation! Life took on a new perspective. Sue and Donny were the most practical and energetic young people imaginable. Kind, sensitive and country-loving, they were positive and cheerful, ready to turn their hand to anything, from pulling weeds in the kale, to driving heavy lorries and tractors and still managing to do the washing-up and help to get the House straight.

My mother, even pre-war, had laughingly complained that our cows had electricity from a diesel-driven generator, but not our House. It is sad that she did not live to see the electricity supply connected in 1948. I well remember the thrill of pressing the light switch for the first time and the bulb lighting up; electricity made the House so much easier to live in. Thanks to the kind expertise of our friend, Sir Claud Hagart-Alexander, even the winding of the turret clock was taken over by electricity through computer-controlled motors. Previously, Sue, who is fond of clocks, had climbed the back stairs daily to the top floor of the House to wind the clock.

Gradually I was becoming a farmer, learning as I worked. Jack was my salvation in this area. Small but wiry and strong, his face weather-beaten and rather drawn, Jack Whyborn was the carter/foreman, responsible for the three cart horses – two Suffolk Punches and a Shire – and for getting the work done on a day-to-day basis, including directing the two tractor drivers.

In my father's words, Jack Whyborn was 'one of nature's gentlemen'. He had a profound knowledge of all aspects of farm work and cultivations and was a skilled craftsman. A good ploughman, Jack could build and thatch a rick, hoe and single sugar beet, carry out all cultivations, knowing instinctively what operation would produce the right tilth. There was no job that Jack could not do well, yet he was a very modest man. I had to lean on Jack, for my own knowledge was scant and he carried me through those early years, never once showing up my ignorance. Jack would quietly say: 'If I were you, I think I would plough that field again.' Or: 'I think the discs will get it right.' 'Carry on Jack' was my watch-word and I shall always be grateful to him.

Sadly for us, after two years, Jack left reluctantly to please his wife, to a 'better' job near a town, which proved quite unsuitable. Jack was too proud to ask to come back to Loseley and by the time we found him again he was riddled with arthritis, depressed and unable to work. He died shortly afterwards and I continue to mourn that the debt of gratitude owed by Loseley to Jack can never be repaid.

All through my active years, I have worked part-time on the Farm at peak periods such as haymaking and harvest. Increasingly I had to spend more and more time dealing with the business side and activities, as well as outside duties, but nothing gives quite the same satisfaction as manual work on the land: pitching sheaves of corn onto wagons, finishing off in the dusk, a mutual sense of achievement in a job well done, usually washed down with beer in the field.

Donny, the first of the Bellinger sisters that I had met, continued her work as professional tennis coach at girls' schools and some secretarial work as well as being a tremendous help and encouragement to me, getting the office sorted out and turning her able hands to anything needed. Her sister, Sue, had spent most the the war driving a YMCA tea van, having failed to get a flying job with the ATA owing to poor maths performance. Sue still possesses the steel helmet with which she was presented, picturing a red cup of tea with the inscription 'Sweet Sue': sadly she declines to place it appropriately alongside the armour in the Great Hall. Sue was helping on the Farm, driving tractors, delivering the milk and helping wherever the greatest need arose. Lovely, fair-haired, slim, with a wonderful sunny disposition, Sue usually sang at the top of her voice while working; and one could hear her several fields away above the noise of her tractor. She also sang when doing the washing up, always happy and smiling; she was an outdoor girl and, like Donny, loved Loseley and its natural beauty, even in its run-down state. Sue was a great animal-lover and knew much more about birds than I ever will. She disabused me of the belief, implanted by Nanny in childhood, that there were no male wrens, Cock Robin having married Jenny Wren. I really believed that!

As well as all the work at Loseley, I had fulfilled my childhood ambition to run a company: Guildcrete Limited manufactured concrete products on the Estate. Sue enjoyed driving but will never forget one day in the hard winter of 1947 driving the Guildcrete six-ton lorry with a full load of concrete blocks and getting stuck on frozen snow going up Haslemere Hill. Another delivery job the following May was a happier one. I was with Sue in a van delivering concrete floor tiles to a friend at Hartley Wintney; the sun shone from a clear blue sky and on the way, beyond Farnham, we paused in a lay-by and I asked her to marry me. To my relief and everlasting joy she said 'Yes'. We were married in Compton Church in October that year and again the sun shone from a clear blue sky. Donny and Sue's friend Willow were bridesmaids and the Farm and Estate staff formed an archway of raised hoes and pitchforks as we came down the church path. Three years later our son Mike was born, a time of rejoicing for us and for the future of Loseley.

In the early days, among all the other jobs, Sue and I looked after the poultry. When we started, the hens were in twelve fold units with twenty-five hens per unit. The folds comprised slatted sleeping quarters with nest boxes, and an area some 12ft by 5ft, wooden sided with wire netting top, so that the hens could exercise and peck on the grass. This was very healthy and it did the grass a lot of good with the scratching and the poultry manure. For us it was very laborious, as the folds had to be moved daily to fresh grass. The water trough also had to be removed daily and cleaned. Grain was scattered on the grass and the mash hopper filled: in frosty weather we gave them hot water in the mash. The eggs had to be collected and in wet weather they were covered in mud. At night the door to the sleeping compartment was shut as precaution against foxes. These three hundred hens took us over an hour a day, excluding egg washing. It was a great relief when we discovered the new henyard system and converted an old horse hovel in which five hundred hens were kept in much greater comfort and the eggs were clean. We had a more comfortable time too and it was altogether more efficient and the birds laid more eggs. The next stage to the henyard, some years later, was deep litter housing, on straw at a density of 3 sq. ft per bird which enabled us to expand to three thousand birds producing hatching eggs.

By this time I had long since given up being part-time poultryman and we were fortunate in finding an expert, most conscientious poultryman, David Lee. After he had been with us a short while we noticed that a van was often parked outside David's cottage, bearing a sticker: 'Don't hesitate – vaccinate!' It was, it turned out, driven by Thelma, a young lady on the Buxted staff who came to check on the health of the flock. No doubt she vaccinated the birds without hesitation. David was shy and did hesitate, but he got her in the end. Years later David and Thelma emigrated for a time to British Columbia and Sue, Mike and I met up with them with Mick and Gee English and our hosts in Vancouver, Gee's brother Jimmy and his wife Muriel.

Soon after getting started with poultry we got going with pigs, breeding Large Whites. Catalina was our favourite sow, a real character, who knew what she wanted and did not consider herself inferior to any human being. To compensate for any awkwardness, she was an excellent mother and very hardy. At first the sows were running loose in a four-acre field called the Ice House. Adjoining the pond, it once accommodated the 'refrigerator' for the House. In Elizabethan times, ice on the pond was broken up and packed into the ice house in the winter and all perishable food was stored there. Although until 1948 we did not have electricity in the House, we did have a paraffin refrigerator.

The sows enjoyed rootling in the sandy soil of the Ice House field and they had plenty of cover, with brambles and bushes as well as a shed. One day I was given the task by the vet of taking a sow's temperature. One does not put the thermometer under the pig's tongue – it's the other end! She certainly could run and made full use of all the bushes and brambles to impede me as I followed full-pelt, trying to get her into the shed, brandishing the thermometer. I finally decided that if she could run like that, there could not be much wrong with her, and after the excitement of the chase the sow apparently forgot that she was ill! In retrospect hilarious, but at the time frustrating because of the time wasted: there was so much to do. I always felt under pressure; even in later years, when on the Farm I felt guilty at being away from Guildway (as Guildcrete later came to be called), and when at Guildway during peak farming periods I had the feeling that I should have been on the Farm.

Now it was time to engage a full-time pigman and his name was Bruce. Bruce was proud of his pigs and persuaded me to enter two young boars for the local show. To parade a cow in the ring is easy: you put a halter on the animal's head and lead it on a short rope. Pigs are different. Bruce presented me with a wooden shield about 2ft 6ins square and a 'bat' 3ft 6ins by 2ins. He then unleashed the young boar, completely untrained. The idea is to direct the boar round the ring, guiding him with the shield in front, and keeping up momentum with the bat to the rear. The young boar thought this a great game. We did get into the ring because he was keen to meet the other young boars already parading there; then the fun started. It was reminiscent of the pursuit of the sow with the thermometer, except that this time I had a large audience to enjoy my discomfiture. Fortunately I was rather more efficient in my other farming operations and I made sure that we never again entered pigs at agricultural shows.

Sue, with help from her mother and Donny, was getting the House and furniture into much better shape. The girls composed some verses on the Loseley situation, which included:

> At the head of us all, to keep us in line
> And teach us what everything means,
> Whose horses and dogs are the joy of his life
> Is the General, late of the Queens.

> We work on the land
> And Oh boy are we tanned
> For we only have baths once a week!

'Baths once a week' was a fact in the early days; one had to put the kettle on the stove and bring it up to the bathroom. The bathroom door, instead of a lock, had a large ENGAGED notice hung on it. We had a number of overseas visitors in those days and each one added ENGAGED in his own language: we even had it in Urdu script. There was no excuse for opening the door when the sign was in place and this trust was never abused. One kind long-term visitor knocked on the door offering a cup of tea. He was quite upset when he was thanked by the girl in the bath but requested to leave the cup outside the door, which he dutifully did. Baths were a luxury and in the summer evenings, after working on the Farm, one of our occasional recreations was swimming either at Cut Mill Ponds or in the rather muddy Loseley lake.

Various friends and Scandinavian students joined us from time to time to help on the Farm. One Swedish boy, Sten Hogbom, arrived from the station by taxi one evening. As we went out to greet him, the taxi was taking him off again, having decided that Loseley was an empty ruin and no one could possibly live there! Memories like this remind us that we have made progress on the challenge. Yesterday, as I write, a large number of people went round the House as paying visitors and there was a wedding reception in the Barn and on the lawn. Eight members of the family are now living at Loseley and it is also a Christian Centre: a far cry from an empty ruin!

From 1946 to 1948 my father and I lived in the main wing of the House and Helen did the cooking and helped, or hindered, according to her mood. Sue and Donny lived with their mother in the Victorian Nursery Wing. A distant cousin, Fletcher, recently divorced, was staying with us. Fletcher, then in his early 40s, was a character straight out of the Victorian era. Of medium build and moustached, Fletcher was kind and most courteous, a bit pompous and plagued with bad luck, or sometimes bad judgment, with financial matters and with women. Fletcher was always prepared to help with any jobs, but he was nocturnal, rising late and going to bed very late. One morning I was impressed to find Fletcher emerging from the bathroom at 6.30am, as I was entering: in those days I started off the Farm staff at 7am. I congratulated Fletcher on his early rising. A few days later he recounted in my presence his amusement at the incident: Fletcher had been on his way to bed; not, as I had assumed, getting up!

Sleeping in the top floor bedrooms but not eating in the House were a number of German and Italian prisoners of war, including Alfred Hempel, a good solid German farmer, who had had a hard time fighting on the Russian front. Alfie was very sound and adaptable, worked on the Farm and assisted with the cows and the garden. He stayed on and happily married Astrid, one of the Swedish girls who came and helped on the domestic side: she was an excellent cook and Alfie never shed any of his weight.

Thinking back to those early years, all the work, the discomfort, no electrics, no heat, the lack of money . . . but they were happy days, unique, never to be seen again. I cannot remember any quarrelling or trouble between any of us; a few irritations but many, many laughs. Most of the helpers were unpaid, working for their keep and experience. As Donny points out: 'If we needed any money we picked some daffodils or something and sold them to a Guildford florist.' It was a happy, hard-working community atmosphere with a challenging goal. Everything had to earn its keep at Loseley, the cellars sprouting potatoes, the top floor housing

PoWs, the moat irrigating the garden, the pond irrigating the early potatoes, the garden producing organic vegetables for sale, the daffodils in the drive going to the florists. No time or money for self-indulgence or pretty bits.

Warmly welcomed weekend visitors in this period and until Meryn died some twenty-five years later, were Meryn and Gwen Lewis who lived in London. Meryn was our solicitor, friend and adviser. A small, sensitive Welshman, he was so conscientious and hard-working, as concerned for the survival of Loseley as I was and even more worried about it. He was a great nature lover and more than anything on his visits here enjoyed going off to the woods on his own to stand and watch and listen. Listening to a pigeon, he interpreted: 'Take two coos Taffy.' A rook passed overhead and Meryn replied: 'Caw caw' to its call. Loseley owes so much to Meryn and we will meet him again in a later chapter.

John Charlton, who as a young officer had been with me in the war, was another member of the household in our first year. John was tall, sensitive, a rather shy person though a real friend to all of us. John shared our enthusiasms; he was a great worker, helping generally, pulling endless dungweed in the kale, clearing timber, getting rid of the clutter of the ages from outbuildings, digging over couch-infested borders, attacking with rotary mower areas of grass unmown for years. Trying to recall John's sayings, Sue said: 'He laughed almost more than he talked.' He was so good-natured. When John left to go to agricultural college we were all sad and I suspect that the Bellinger girls were to miss him even more than I did. We had been a relaxed and happy foursome with no nonsenses to place stress on our relationships: we were too busy. One day John would return and that is another chapter.

Young Danes and Swedes stayed and worked happily with us, students widening their experience and improving their English. We are grateful to them all and we share happy memories of those far-off days, including Sten, Brita, Anders, Anita, Cecilia, Dr Jan, Ulla and Addi, Jonna and Jorgen and their grown-up children. From England we should mention Avril and Sheila Darnton, David Wenham and elegant Robert Sanders who helped with the pigs!

The one person who seemed unlikely ever to leave was Helen, the Hungarian. She might be difficult to get rid of, so we thought. One day I happened to be in the kitchen when Helen, unprovoked, started hurling abuse at me, picked up a large sharp-pointed kitchen knife and lunged at me. I grabbed her arms; although thick-set and quite active, she was not strong and I pushed her up against the wall and banged her against it. All the time Helen was screaming abuse at the top of her voice.

At this moment, when I was fighting with Helen, we had a rare visitor. We seldom had visitors: the House was over a mile from the main road, the drive badly pot-holed and we were too busy for socialising. Business callers came to the Estate Office. This visitor did not ring the bell, he walked straight in. He would have heard Helen screaming and, being a policeman, he did not waste time over courtesies. A policeman? I had not telephoned: no one had telephoned, and the onslaught on me had only started a minute before, so even if someone had phoned they could not have had a response as quickly as that. Our visitor was not only a policeman but a detective superintendent and he knew – which we did not – that Helen had a record. He asked no questions, ordered Helen to pack her bags, bundled her into his car and we did not see her again until forty years later. The officer had come without an appointment to talk about coaching for the Loseley Park Cricket Club. He could not have chosen a more significant moment: the odds against that happening must be millions to one against. Just a happy coincidence?

Meanwhile I was learning all I could about farming and estate management, not only from Jack and my Farm chaps but from various business advisers, some of my tenant farmers and other friends in the business. I assiduously read all the farming and landowning magazines, went on Farm walks and attended lectures and discussions.

Farm walks were very friendly and helpful occasions organised by the local National Farmers' Union or other farming societies. They were hosted by local farmers who told us about their farms, crops and stock. This was usually followed by a tour of the farm, on foot or on tractor-drawn trailers, and details were given about the crops and stock as we went round. Afterwards talk and questions flowed over sandwiches, cakes and ale, kindly provided by the hosts. It was also a social occasion and several wives would be present. I do not believe that other industries have anything to match farm walks; they were a great help to a newcomer like me and in years to come we were glad of the opportunity of returning some of the hospitality we had received.

In those days farming was regarded as a way of life as well as one's livelihood. A farmer would spend time leaning on the gate, watching his cattle, assessing their condition, looking for 'bad doers' – cows that were too thin, coughing or their coats lifeless; 'bullers' – coming on heat. The farmer would walk his pastures: does this field need harrowing, should it be grazed or left for silage, does it need more nitrogen?

A book which influenced me was George Henderson's *The Farming Ladder*. George and Frank Henderson were hard-working farmers on a small acreage, perfectionists who believed the secret of success to be 'Work, muck, thought' and the three great evils 'Smoking, swearing, standing about'. One quoted adage that I found helpful in business was: 'Find an opportunity in every difficulty, not a difficulty in every opportunity.' Widely acclaimed at the time, *The Farming Ladder* is not considered relevant by farmers in these days of chemical farming, ever bigger, more powerful machines and large units. 'Work' and 'Muck' are no longer praiseworthy and 'Thought' is too often governed by the computer and the 'bottom line'. Much of the craft and the joy has gone from farming in this profit-orientated, high-tech era.

In my first year at home I was elected as Churchwarden of St Nicholas Church, Compton. I was also elected to Artington Parish Council, on which I have now served for over forty-eight years, and to various farming organisations and the St John Council for Surrey and then the Surrey County Agricultural Executive Committee. My parents had both been members of Guildford RDC but I declined to stand: I did not have the time.

Social life was almost non-existent in the first few years, there were few days off and no holidays beyond a very occasional weekend. Not only was there so much to be done but Loseley was such a fascinating challenge that somehow one did not want to go away. A holiday would have almost been an anti-climax and we did not wish to spend money on ourselves or to do anything to inflate the overdraft.

Early days are important. Those times were tough and often uncomfortable, the House was cold, we worked long and hard and were tired out at the end of the day. There was harmony and unity of purpose, conscious of working for a cause greater than self: like the just-ended war years. We were always planning and dreaming of new ventures and challenges ahead. Loseley was

a challenge bigger than ourselves and we *did* put Loseley first and
before our own convenience. Gradually Loseley was responding
and what had begun as a grim duty became a labour of love.
At that time my relationship with God could also be regarded
as in the 'Duty' phase and the transition from duty to love came
a few years later. It occurred, surprisingly, as a result of realising
my childhood ambition to run a company.

CHAPTER 3

COMPANY LTD

Some children dream of becoming engine drivers, some firemen: I had always wanted to run a company. I put 'Co. Ltd' after my name at the age of 6; I wrote it on an old Wimbledon Tennis Tournament ticket that had been given to me as a plaything and stuck it on my door. I did not know what it meant but I had seen 'Co. Ltd' after names on the back of lorries and it looked exciting. As far as I know, I had never met anyone in business: my father was a retired Brigadier General and my mother's father was an Admiral: business was not in the blood!

I first realised my ambition to run my own business at the age of 9, using the school's only currency of sweets – 'tuck'. Unaware that I was following in Sir William More's steps with his Lottery involvement in 1567 and anticipating HM government by some sixty-five years, I regret to say that the venture was the Harecroft Hall Sweepstake. I remember the growing pile of sweets getting very sticky before being distributed to the winners. The 'profit' was re-invested in buying second-hand books, which formed a lending library.

I clearly recall a conversation in the Yellow Dormitory at Harecroft Hall with my friend Charles Wylie. 'What are you going to do when you grow up, Charles?' 'I'm going to be a Gurkha Officer.' 'What's a Gurkha?' 'They're little men from Nepal and they're wonderful fighters. My father was a Gurkha Colonel. How about you, James?' Without hesitation I responded: 'I'm going to run a company.' At the time we were both about 10 years old. Charles did become a Gurkha Officer and had a distinguished career and we shall meet him again at a later stage.

Later, at Eton, books again formed the basis of my business. In partnership with a friend, Derek Hubbard, we bought used lesson books at the end of each half (term), stored them in our rooms during the holidays and sold them on the first day of the next half. On the first day of one half in 1937 we made a profit of £5 – equivalent to a very much larger sum today. Profits were re-invested, this time in a printing press, which was squeezed into my little room. Unfortunately in those days business initiative was not encouraged and at the end of 1937 the school authorities and my parents took the view that things had gone far enough and we were closed down, regrettably but without ill-will.

These early business ventures had been fun things, and I obtained probably more satisfaction through building up and operating the business than in anything else during my school years. I suspect that I never quite got rid of this amateur attitude to business and some accountants later despaired of me. Nowadays people regard business primarily as 'making money'. Although Loseley desperately needed money, it is a strange fact that I never put profitability first. For me it was a creative urge, presumably akin to that felt by a painter or poet. Building a business is creative and satisfying, more so if the motives are deeper than money.

As soon as I left school, I turned my mind to generating business at Loseley. I still have a letter from the Metal Box Company Ltd dated 15th September 1938, the month I left Eton, in response to my request for information on canning potatoes. I replied to Metal Box thanking them for the information supplied, adding: 'The idea is to make the Estate pay. Times being bad, I do not want to spend much money on something that will not pay its way. We could also grow tomatoes, peas and beans and can them on a small scale with existing garden customers as a start, with a hand sealer.' Canning organic vegetables remains an unfulfilled ambition, although in 1948 we did purchase some cans and a small can sealer from Metal Box and successfully canned tomatoes, but not in commercial quantities.

The war intervened and in 1947 it was concrete houses that got in the way of the vegetable canning project. I mentioned in the last chapter cousin Fletcher and his misfortunes. One day Fletcher told me about Mr Morrison and his house. Morrison, a retired Burmah railway engineer, had invented a concrete panel housing system which, he claimed, would resolve the country's post-war housing shortage. Morrison lived in a prototype house and had formed a company. Having persuaded Fletcher to invest a considerable sum in the project, Morrison was living off this capital and doing nothing about producing houses. For me, just out of the army and with the ignorance and enthusiasm of youth, the idea of setting up a factory to produce much-needed housing was irresistible. 'Let's go and see Morrison and his house,' I suggested to Fletcher and off we went.

Concrete houses are not beautiful neither are they warm; worse still, Morrison's house had a flat roof and flat roofs are apt to leak. Despite all this, Morrison was persuasive and I was keen to get the business going. Morrison came to Loseley and we showed him the site on the Estate accommodating a small fencing business, with a spare building and acres of land for expansion. I invited Philip Yatman, the owner of the fencing business, to meet Morrison; he came but was too wise and experienced to accept my offer of participation. Minor details such as capital were not even considered. I decided to go ahead. There was a long delivery on three special gear wheels required for the gantry to be built for lifting and loading the four-ton panels, so these were put on order with a Huddersfield firm and several months later arrived in the Loseley farmyard.

I invited a friend from army days, Mick English, who had married my Canadian-born cousin, Gee, to join me in the venture. Mick had been my Squadron second-in-command and could be relied upon to enliven most proceedings with humour, sardonic comment or ditty; only occasionally did he lapse into a morose mood. Gee was a wonderful girl, petite, dark and full of commonsense, always helpful and remarkably patient; she had come over to England before the war from her home in British Columbia to stay with my grandmother and Aunt Grace in their house two miles from Loseley. Having no capital, and to the best of my memory, without any commitment on salary, Mick bravely gave up his job in a small engineering firm to come and join me.

Before going further we enlisted the help of the Cement and Concrete Association to advise on the feasibility of the housing project. Mr Baumgarten, the executive assigned to us, was a very practical and friendly person but to our dismay, after careful assessment of the project, Mr Baumgarten gave it an unqualified thumbs-down. Apart from other technical horrors, as an engineer Morrison must have known that four-ton concrete panels cannot be lifted and loaded twenty-four hours after casting, and Mick and

I should have realised this. That was a bad moment and Mick had given up his job to join me.

Next day we again rang Mr Baumgarten: 'In the light of your report we cannot proceed with making concrete houses but there must be other things that we can make in concrete. May we come and see you?' We went up to London and Mr Baumgarten produced details of the Hartcrete concrete block machine from Denmark which produced cavity concrete blocks in two sizes, equivalent to two bricks plus mortar course and four bricks plus mortar course. The two-brick size could be laid with one hand just like a brick, with a trowel in the other hand, in theory doubling the productivity of a brick layer. That seemed easier than making four-ton concrete panels.

We placed the order for the machine, purchased an ancient 10/7 Stothert & Pitt petrol-driven concrete mixer and then realised we needed planning consent for the factory. Fortunately this was forthcoming quite quickly from Guildford RDC but only for a six months provisional period! I learned long afterwards that the view was taken that we knew nothing about business or concrete and that we were unlikely to survive for six months. We only just proved them wrong.

We purchased two secondhand Nissen huts and advertised for workers. Dick James applied for the key job of mixer driver. Heavily built, red-cheeked, Dick proved a splendid choice; sound and conscientious, he was soon promoted to foreman and stayed with us until he died. His wife became our tea lady and one of their sons joined the firm years later. With the help of Pop Reeve, the Loseley maintenance foreman, Dick and the newly recruited labour force, including German PoWs, erected the Nissen huts and a shed and put down concrete roadways. So much for six months' provisional planning consent! Mick and I mucked in and I remember blisters on my hands from hours of tamping concrete.

It was an exciting moment when our six-ton Austin lorry arrived, with 'Guildcrete Ltd' on headboard, and name, address and products on tailboard. I also remember the thrill of the first six-ton delivery of cement followed by the start-up of production on 17th June 1947. A young Danish engineer came to set up the block machine, adding ENGAGED in Danish for the bathroom door, and we recruited an Irishman, Paddy, as the operator. We really were in business: it did not matter that we were producing concrete blocks instead of houses. I did not know it at the time but houses by the thousand would eventually pass out of that factory.

We had advertised for 'Two tall men for concrete block factory': the height was needed to reach the top racks of the drying frames. One of the tall men who applied was Hugh Streeter, well educated and immediately taken on as company secretary/sales manager/book-keeper/typist. We could not have done better and Hugh remained with us for many years. Soon we had to turn our attention to boosting sales: stocks, and with them the overdraft, were beginning to grow. We widened the product range by producing concrete paving slabs, floor tiles, fence posts and garden edging. An advertisement in the local paper ran:

> IF THE THOUGHT OF BUILDING SHOCKS
> YOU CAN'T HAVE SEEN OUR GUILDCRETE BLOCKS
> SLABS AND TILES AND FENCE POSTS TOO
> PERMIT-FREE ARE MADE FOR YOU!

I do not think that the verse by the Bellinger girls made much impact, but the lines have stayed in my head for over forty-five years.

After a few months came an unexpected problem: a letter from a customer complaining about cracks in a wall built with our blocks. Mr Baumgarten had told us about problems with curing concrete, but he had not told us that concrete expands and contracts. The movement has to be allowed for, either by providing expansion joints or by using a weak mortar mix. This was our first real complaint and our first technical problem; we realised the seriousness of the situation and we satisfied the customer. From then on we sent to all customers the correct specification to be used for the mortar mix.

We had not realised that manufacturing is a far more complex operation than running a trading or service company and technical problems are certain to occur from time to time. With manufacturing comes the management of the factory with its machines, the production team, production control, quality control, material and stock control, plant maintenance, product development, safety, design and many other factors in addition to the commercial, marketing and sales functions. We did jump in at the deep end of business.

It had been agreed that Mick should be Managing Director, with no financial stake in the company. I was unpaid Chairman and assisted as far as my heavy Loseley commitments permitted. As an office we shared a hut with Alf Burchell, foreman of the fencing company with which we shared the site. Alf, small and cheerful, always helpful and sound and never complaining, as well he might, at having his office taken over; the lychgate Alf constructed in 1934 is now re-erected at Loseley as a memorial to him. There were no chairs in the office, just a built-in ledge in front of the window as the desk, with an upright telephone and one tall wooden stool for the tall Hugh Streeter.

One morning when I came into the office I was shocked to find a note to me from Mick saying that I had obviously lost confidence in him and that he had decided to leave forthwith. The problem arose because I had queried Mick's costings on the concrete blocks. I had put up the capital and we were now losing money. I did feel, as Chairman, that the costing needed checking. I think we both realised, being new to business and civilian life, that this was part of the learning curve; it seemed unlikely that the business would be able to pay Mick a significant salary for some time and it was probably sensible to part company at this stage.

Mick and Gee emigrated to Canada and Mick joined the lumber company Macmillan Bloedell, where he stayed until his eventual retirement. By a strange coincidence, many years after Mick joined them, Macmillans became one of our main timber suppliers, so Mick English and I were doing business together again, this time in timber and separated by some eight thousand miles.

In the course of our parting talk Mick had dropped the remark: 'I am concerned that the chaps in the works don't like you and most of them will leave when I go.' I was amazed and shocked by this statement and determined to disprove it; in fact no one left and we quickly established an excellent rapport. The men had been responsible to Mick as Managing Director while I had spent most of my time on the Farm; at Guildcrete, as Chairman, I was concerned with building up the business, rather than with the workforce, who were Mick's responsibility. Although at the time offended by the comment, I later realised that it was the most helpful and constructive thing that Mick could have said.

From that moment I always ensured keeping in close touch with the chaps who worked with us. We are proud of our record in 'labour relations' and our philosophy of teamwork and sharing profits and information has paid off.

I had achieved my childhood ambition of running my own business and I found it immensely satisfying. I never had problems with the chaps at Guildcrete: we had open, frank discussions and official works meetings and these continued for nearly forty years. We later introduced profit sharing which further consolidated the teamwork which had been built up.

After Mick left in 1948 my father joined me as non-Executive Director. I ran the firm as Chairman and Managing Director, until handing over my MD role to Fred Gooch in 1972, serving forty-seven years as Chairman. Guildcrete gradually expanded; the range of products steadily increased, and further growth came through contracts for local authority housing components including coping, chimney caps, fencing and paving. Staff increased to keep pace including a works manager/estimator and a book-keeper, and there were promotions from the shop floor to chargehand. We also took on two carpenters as mould makers: one of these, John Sillence, is still with Guildway in 1995, and the other, Tom Enticknap Jnr, is now retired.

The six months planning consent for our factory had fortunately been extended and every year or two we made new applications for factory or office extensions and other facilities. Most of these were granted although we were constantly reminded that we were in the Green Belt. Very sensibly, after a few years, Guildford RDC concluded that we were there to stay and we were requested to draw up a ten-year plan for the site. Our dealings with the local authority and county council were open and harmonious and have remained so.

Money had always been a problem because there was virtually none, except what the Westminster Bank kindly lent us. We had little security, for the Estate was mortgaged and we were always near our overdraft limit. I always told the Bank what I believed to be the facts and never misled them: I find no merit in deviousness. This policy paid off and I have always been trusted. Loyalty is another commodity which has paid off for me. At one time in the early 1980s I was overdrawn £1,600,000 on Guildway and £250,000 on Loseley and I am still with NatWest after fifty-five years.

One day, about to enter the office, I was pulled aside by one of the staff and hustled to the back entrance. Inside the front door was a rough-looking scrap merchant, demanding the money we owed for some steel reinforcement bars. He got paid in the end, as did all our suppliers, and in the years ahead I was to have plenty of experience in dealing with creditors and financial crises. It was a period in which one discovered one's true friends and, even more significant, it was to bring me closer to God. Meanwhile, at present my priority must be Loseley and the farming.

CHAPTER 4

THE LOSELEY CO-PARTNERSHIP

It was a satisfying challenge, building up the Guildcrete business, working things out with the men in the factory, forming close relationships with customers, suppliers, the bank manager and others. I was learning as I worked – about business, finance, people and technicalities. The same at Loseley, learning about farming, management, finance, people and acquiring a wide range of vital knowhow. The great need was to create income so that the House and Estate could be put into good order.

We expanded the farming, taking on more land whenever a tenant left. We added the pig unit and turkeys and expanded the hens, we built up the Jersey herd from some seventy head to over eight hundred at peak and we added a flock of sheep. We expanded the arable and increased the potatoes to forty acres, installing an irrigation system with the lake as the reservoir. Early seed potatoes were 'chitted' (sprouted) in the cellars of Loseley House under fluorescent lights. The early potatoes were my favourite crop; it was vital to have them ready to dig as early as possible as the price was high in early June but fell rapidly when other farmers in the area started lifting. We planted the earlies on south sloping light land and we did all we could to get the crop earlier, including choice of variety, planting date, irrigation, seed chitting. We were sometimes the first farm in the area to start lifting potatoes. We tended to make a good profit on our earlies and we also had the benefit, after the potatoes were lifted in June/July, of sowing a 'catch crop' of rape or other feed for the cows for autumn grazing before the field was ploughed for winter wheat. Two crops harvested and another sown all in the space of nine months was both satisfying and profitable.

In 1946, the standard agricultural wage was £4 per forty-eight-hour week and most workers were housed rent-free in tied cottages.

'Agricultural labourers' was a term I resented and would never use. Most agricultural workers were craftsmen, many skilled in a wide range of crafts as well as being well versed in countryside lore and in the ways of wildlife. There were some great characters, as well as a few awkward ones. Families stuck together. The bicycle was the means of personal transport; alternatively walk a mile or more to the bus stop. A taxi, on the agricultural wage, was for emergencies only. Some wives, understandably, yearned for the town. The nearest shop and pub to Loseley were nearly two miles away. Life was hard for Farm workers in those days. By contrast, his counterpart today has so many advantages over his town cousin. Living in the country, he has a modernised cottage with TV, hi-fi, garden, car and probably a garage to put it in. Farm workers have all the benefits of the countryside like the commuters, but without the stress of commuting.

I mentioned earlier that four soldiers came back to join my father after the First World War. They were: his batman, George Neville, as butler; Harry Hedger, transport corporal, as carter; Pop Reeves, pioneer sergeant, as maintenance foreman; and Tesch, orderly room sergeant, as Estate Office clerk. They formed a splendid, loyal staff backbone. Neville, Harry and Pop remained for the rest of their lives and two of Pop's sons also spent their working lives at Loseley, Les as maintenance foreman and Tom as gardener. A third son, Colin, also did a splendid job as tractor driver foreman before transferring to be head groundsman of a local golf club. Harry's daughter, Teresa, also worked for much of her life at Loseley, the last few years on the Dairy Products computer. Fred Nash, the woodman, joined us in 1947 and remained at Loseley for the rest of his life. Fred's son, David, has worked for Guildcrete ever since leaving school and David's son, Paul, also joined Guildcrete from school, three generations of a fine family. Although his official title was head woodman, Fred had a go at just about every job at Loseley, including unpopular ones such as hand-spreading smelly fish manure, as well as hoeing and singling, hay, silage, grass drying and harvest carting. He also acted as relief milk roundsman. His stock expression was 'We'll get there' and, with Fred's help, we did.

In the year of my return to Loseley, hints were dropped by a tenant farmer that I could be in danger of dispossession under the wartime regulations still in force due to the presence of 'notifiable weeds', still rather too visible in some fields. Happily I did not even receive an official warning and within a year or two I was appointed to be a member of the committee which decided on dispossessions – the Surrey War Agricultural Executive Committee. Little did I imagine in those traumatic early days that in 1984 I would be awarded the RASE Bledisloe Gold Medal for Landowners. But there was much to be done before then.

We had a good team of workers, but things did not always go smoothly. Tom Enticknap had joined Loseley on leaving school and was in his early 30s when I returned after the war. Tom was a very conscientious tractor driver, who took pride in his tractor, which ran on TVO fuel but had to be switched to petrol for starting. During busy periods I used to take over driving Tom's tractor during the lunch hour. Tom did not reckon much on this and if I was just a minute late, Tom would stop the engine and so arrange the fuel taps that I would have difficulty in re-starting. There was no self-starter in those days and there were moments when I was not pleased with Tom.

Mick's remark about the chaps at Guildcrete not wanting to work for me had galvanised me to action and led to a good relationship with everyone who worked there. Unexpectedly, something similar happened at Loseley. One day in 1950 my secretary reported that one of the chaps had said to her: 'The mean old so-and-so has bought himself a Land Rover but is too mean to pay us overtime on sugar beet singling.' This comment alerted me to the fact that our communications were poor. I was determined to put this right. The Land Rover had been bought, on hire purchase, primarily for use on the Farm for haulage, drawing wagons and shooting rabbits at night in the fields where crops were suffering from rabbit damage. This was an investment for the Farm, whereas beet singling had been stopped because it was taking too long and was uneconomic at overtime rates.

I got all the men together in the old carpenter's shop, where they had their morning break, and told them the facts: 'We are going through a very difficult period. I have had to take out a mortgage on the Estate, we have a large bank overdraft and we are not yet making enough profit to cover our costs. If things do not improve we shall all be out on our ears – you and me; we shall have to sell up. I am sure you don't want that any more than I do. We must all pull together and I would like to hold regular meetings with you to share the information with you and get your ideas, and I will give you a 15 per cent share of any profit. It is up to you: I shall not force this on you. Hands up those in favour.'

The men were 100 per cent in favour and showed great enthusiasm for the proposal. Tom, the 'difficult' tractor driver, said: 'This is what we have been waiting for' and he went on to clock up a record sixty-four years of Loseley service, including working part-time after retirement until the age of 84.

The Loseley Co-Partnership commenced on 1st January 1951. The details were set out in a booklet issued to every individual, stating the object as being 'To give all a real interest in their work and a sense of partnership in the business. To encourage and reward greater output and to share the benefits of any economies achieved.' All adult workers with over one year's service had equal shares in the total profit. Over the years we made small adjustments and geared bonus shares to salary, but it remained on the basis of total profit, not departmental, to foster teamwork and collaboration between departments: it was for the wellbeing of Loseley as a whole.

The scheme transformed our relationship far beyond my expectations. Many of the workers had much more detailed knowledge of their respective spheres than I did. Previously they were not worried if they got delayed in their operations, perhaps by a machine getting stuck in some narrow gateway. Now they asked for the gateway to be widened and anything wasting time they wanted rectified. The men reported various forms of waste that they had noticed and which could be prevented, they suggested alternatives to the cropping programme in order to make better use of the fields, they pointed out ways of reducing breakages, increasing yields, saving time. Journalists and broadcasters who from time to time attended meetings of the Loseley Co-Partnership were impressed by the attitude and by the bright ideas which the chaps put forward. At least one journalist commented that he had heard more sensible contributions from the members at the meeting than at many a City board meeting. That was good for morale, although I suspect that some of our members did not have very high expectations of what transpired in City boardrooms!

Surprisingly there was very seldom any mention by members of 'welfare' matters at our meetings, even though the tied cottages which they occupied lacked many amenities back in 1950. I think they realised that they were in a privileged position in sharing the information, which included viewing the accounts, and they were anxious not to abuse it. Even more than their contribution at meetings, it was the way in which the team worked that effected the transformation. In 1959 when I was away for six weeks on business with Fred Gooch in the USA, they made a special effort to ensure that nothing lapsed and that everything was in really good order on my return.

It was farmers, not the workers, who tended to be suspicious and unimpressed. 'Do you really ask your tractor driver's permission to buy him a new tractor?' a farmer asked. 'Yes, he has got to spend his time driving it.' People ask whether the scheme has paid off. My stock answer is: 'If you are proposing to do it just to increase profit, then forget it. I do it because of attitude of mind, regarding the workers as partners.' I can now say that it has paid off. I regard forming the Loseley Co-Partnership as the most important initiative of my business career. With minor alterations, agreed with the membership from time to time over forty-five years, the scheme continues, now under my son's chairmanship. Because of the Co-Partnership's spirit, Loseley Dairy Products, our most profitable enterprise, was born, and that is another chapter.

A short time after forming the Loseley Co-Partnership in 1951, I was approached by Mr Ward Daw, Director of the Industrial Co-Partnership, inviting me to speak at the Annual Convention of the Association. It was encouraging to learn that I was not alone in wanting to share profits and information with the workforce. IPA had hundreds of firms in its membership, including ICI, Rolls Royce, John Lewis, Tate and Lyle. It was daunting to be invited to speak at the Conference but after friendly assurances, I accepted. The title of my talk on that occasion was 'Down To Earth' and I dubbed myself as the Peasant. Sue and I met many interesting and influential people at the Conference, many of whom became friends. I was later elected to the Executive Committee of IPA on which I served for twenty-five years.

I have mentioned the depression I felt during my first weeks on returning to Loseley, with so much that needed doing; already Sue and Donny had made a tremendous contribution together with others who had joined later. Now with the boosted morale of the Co-Partnership, everyone was pulling their weight and I began to feel that we really were going forward.

The Loseley Challenge

By 1952 there was still a formidable backlog of building maintenance and new buildings were required for the expanding Farm enterprises, including poultry housing and a grain store. At about that time Pop Reeves, the maintenance foreman since 1919, was due for retirement. I responded to a 'Situations Wanted' advert in the *CGA Magazine*. Fred Gooch, the applicant, arrived for interview by car – our first job applicant to do so. He brought with him his wife Joan, son Gary and a Lithuanian, Jo Balinonis. Jo was a carpenter working with Mr Gooch on the estate where he was currently employed. We drove round the farms and, with some embarrassment, I led Fred Gooch from one set of crumbling, leaking buildings to another; but he seemed very bright and keen and I hoped very much that he would join us. His father had been a small farmer and master baker in Norfolk and Fred had had to work hard as a boy, often delivering the milk on his way to school and helping on the farm in the evenings.

A week later Fred came back for a final talk and, to my great relief, said: 'I'll take the job. I can see there's plenty of scope!' We agreed the rate of pay at £7 10s per week plus free cottage: overtime at agricultural rate, milk and logs at staff rate, a secondhand bath and cooker/heater to be provided by Loseley and installed by Mr Gooch in his own time.

Fred was right, there was plenty of scope, for almost every building on the Estate still required attention and there was the need for new buildings. But that was only the beginning: Fred was to stay with me for the remainder of his working life and together we would pioneer a new industry. Fred Gooch's arrival was the second big milestone in my Loseley journey, the Bellinger girls being the first.

Fred soon got the pre-1914 rack saw bench operating in the farmyard and produced most of the timber needed for our repairs and construction work. A henyard was constructed and shortly afterwards the 180-ton grain store. At the time this was considered a progressive structure, designed with the assistance of the Ministry of Agriculture County Machinery Adviser. It provided for the storage and drying of grain in bins with electrically heated air propelled by fans through ducts under the bins. The grain was hydraulically tipped from trailers into the reception pit, elevated and mechanically cleaned before being taken by conveyors into the bins. When required, grain for cattle feed was conveyed pneumatically into the loft of a nearby building where it was milled and mixed. Grain could also be blown into an elevated hopper for the rapid bulk loading of lorries. The grain store and the tanker combine harvester purchased the same year revolutionised our harvesting, requiring more technical ability but minimal manual effort and different skills. We did not reduce the workforce because we were gradually increasing our acreage, for as farms fell vacant on the Estate we took them in hand.

I did not realise it then, but my farming career could not have started at a better moment. In 1946 the new agricultural revolution was still in its early stages; progress since has been phenomenal, with many new ideas in addition to mechanisation. In those days farmers were respected for doing a splendid job feeding the nation and saving imports.

In 1946 we still had three cart-horses, Princess and Duke – splendid they looked, great powerful chestnuts, enormous feet, proud yet docile and obedient. These Suffolks did the ploughing and the heavier work; Dick the Shire worked mainly on carting. The corn was cut with a self-binder, which threw out the sheaves of corn after tying them with twine, a fascinating piece of late nineteenth-century mechanical wizardry. The sheaves were stooked by hand – stood upright with four sheaves each side, their heads meeting in the middle to allow the grain to dry out. After a week or more, according to the weather, the sheaves were loaded onto a wagon, then pitched onto ricks. In winter the contractor would pull into the farmyard with his thrashing tackle – steam engine, thrashing drum, baler, fuel tender etc. The sheaves were pitched onto the deck of the machine, the operator cut the strings and fed the sheaves into the drum. Another worker took off the sacks of wheat and stacked them, someone took the straw trusses and pitched them onto a rick and a further member of the team dealt with tail corn, weed seeds and rubbish and kept the site tidy.

Our first combine harvester was a cheaper tractor-drawn model and the corn went into sacks, requiring a man for bagging in addition to the tractor driver. On one occasion when I was doing my turn on bagging on the combine and Tom was driving the tractor, we happened to go over a bad bump as I was removing the filled bag. The bag and I fell off the platform and made a heavy landing. I still remember Tom's relief when he saw that I was moving and more or less intact. We expanded our grain acreage and could then justify a self-propelled tanker combine, which not only eliminated the man taking off the bags but also the end-of-the-day chore of collecting the sacks from the field and tipping them into the granary. Now, the combine harvester augured the grain into trailers which tipped direct into the in-take pit of the new grain store. An amazing transformation had taken place, eliminating all the labours of stooking, throwing out, carting, ricking, threshing, sack handling, to a completely mechanised operation which also greatly reduced the weather risks. It required completely different knowhow and technology from the old system.

An array of labour-saving machines became available which cut out the laborious jobs; these included pick-up balers, potato harvesters, muck loaders and spreaders, forage harvesters. Probably the most significant advance in this era was the Ferguson tractor, with its hydraulic system. Implements could be attached direct to the rear of the tractor, operated by a hydraulic lever. This gave the driver much better control and manoeuvrability than the traditional trailed implements. Apart from ploughs, cultivators and drills, front-mounted loaders could be fitted, which could clean out the dung from a stock yard and load spreaders without any manual effort. It could lift and load sacks, silage and objects weighing up to half a ton. Harry Ferguson's tractors made life on the Farm much easier, saving innumerable strained backs. We were quick to take advantage and soon we had four 'Fergies'. Sue loved driving them and we still enthuse when we spot one of the original little grey tractors.

There have also been tremendous changes in the management of dairy herds during my farming career and productivity has increased tenfold. When I took over in 1946, we had about forty milking cows in two cowsheds. Each cow had a slate hung above its stall on which was written the cow's name, calving date and present cake ration. It was very pleasing to be able to walk along the passageway behind the cows who were contentedly munching the hay or chewing the cud; it was warm and cosy and the cows had nice beds of clean straw to lie on. At milking time the bucket with special lid with rubber pipes attached was brought to each cow in turn. The milk flowed into the bucket and when the flow dried up the teat cups were removed, the milk carried in the bucket to the weighing room, tipped into the weighing bucket, the weight of milk entered on a list, then the milk was taken in the bucket up some steps and poured into the tank which fed through the wall to the cooler in the dairy, where it was bottled or separated into cream. This happened twice daily, in early morning and afternoon.

All food – hay, silage, grains and cattle cake – was conveyed to the cows by hand with pitchfork, barrow or overhead carrier. Everything was so laborious that four cowmen were required to tend some forty milkers plus thirty youngstock and two bulls. Now we have two herds of 130 cows housed in yards, fed by self-unloading wagons discharging into continuous mangers. The cows are milked in parlours in batches, the milk flows direct from the cows into jars and then to the bulk tank where it is cooled. The teat cups are removed automatically when the milk flow ceases. One man now milks 130 cows or more compared with three men milking 40 cows, and the individual yields are up by some 30 per cent.

As there is no grass for cows to graze in winter, some fields have to be reserved for conservation during spring and summer. In the late 1940s on most farms this entailed making hay. The grass would be cut and thrown out to dry by hand-forking. If it did not rain during the next few days, the hay would be hand-forked into cocks (heaps) to give some protection from dew and rain while the drying continued. It was then thrown out again on a sunny day and then forked onto wagons and pitched onto ricks. We stored our hay and straw in a large Dutch barn. One day when Sue and I were on the rick, a spark from the little engine driving the hay elevator ignited the hay and the whole stack was soon an inferno. Fortunately no one was injured, though a young worker who was with us was at first too terrified to get off the rick. Despite the efforts of the fire brigade, ourselves and the Farm staff, the fire was not fully extinguished for twenty-four hours. Even when there are no casualties a fire is an emotional and draining experience; we all felt it and it brought us all closer together. Fortunately the insurance company met the loss claim in full and no reduction in bonus was suffered.

Realising the importance of grassland management for profitable milk production, one of my better ideas, during the spring and summer months, was weekly evening grass walks. Richard Atkin, the head herdsman, Colin Reeve the foreman and I walked round all the grass fields and decided which were to be grazed by the cows, which were to be kept for hay or silage, and we made decisions on topping, harrowing, cutting, fertiliser applications and on re-seeding. The pay-off came in improved efficiency and profit but to my amazement in 1956 we were also awarded the Surrey Grassland Society Cup for the best managed grass in the county. This was a great encouragement and we won it again in 1960.

Richard, Colin and I worked as a team. Richard Atkin – tall, fit and strong with tremendous energy – was the son-in-law of Tom Winser, my father's herdsman during the war years. Richard was very conscientious: nothing was too good for his cows and he worked hard for them and he worked fast. He enjoyed a chat, usually opening with: 'I don't know about you but I always think . . .' Richard's wife Kathleen was a hard worker too, bringing up five children, helping Richard with their garden, helping in the dairy when needed and finishing her working career with Loseley Dairy Products. Richard suffered from lung problems in his later years and had to transfer from the cows to the garden, and sadly he died soon after retirement. Colin, the foreman, was strong, stockily built, with rather auburn hair. He was straight, open, and spoke his mind; he also wrote poetry and it was rumoured that he had a devastating right hook, though I never put this to the test! Colin was a perfectionist on his tractor and everything he did he did well.

Colin and his brother Tom put considerable effort into keeping the cricket pitch in good order, frequently rolling with the heavy roller as well as mowing etc. One day I was with Colin in the cricket field when all eight horses came thundering across the field, right over the precious cricket pitch. All too clearly one could see the damage that the hooves had made. 'That's it!' barked Colin, 'I'm through with looking after the pitch.' No more cricket at Loseley.

The Farm was expanding, becoming more mechanised, more technical and similar developments were happening at Guildcrete, the buildings company, so I had less time available on the Farm and I had to appoint a Farm Manager to run the day-to-day work. In fact, we had a series of Farm Managers, no doubt my own fault for remaining too involved in the farming, and the relationship between the Manager and the Farm staff was not an easy one. Although still directly involved in policy and decision-making on cropping, manuring and other details, I did miss being involved in the farming day-to-day. Sue and I often talk nostalgically of the days when we drove tractors and looked after the hens, though for many years we continued to drive combine harvesters during lunch-breaks and I helped when I could, in the evenings, during harvest time with bale carting as well as bringing round the ice-cream tubs which superseded the beer in later years.

By 1974 we were farming 1,500 acres, including an additional 500 acres rented at Greyfriars on the Hogs Back for five years. We had 800 acres of grain and at peak 800 Jerseys. 1974 must have been my most hectic year, for much of that year of expansion I was acting as Farm Manager and it was also the year in which I was High Sheriff of Surrey, as well as continuing as Executive Chairman of Guildway.

Prior to going on a three-year Farming and Farm Management Course at the Royal Agricultural College, Cirencester, our son Mike was starting his practical farm training, working with the cows at Greyfriars Farm; taking after his grandfather, Mike was naturally good with livestock and the cattle were always his main farming interest. How fortunate we were to have a son who wanted to farm and to join us in working for Loseley and the Estate.

CHAPTER 5

THE ESTATE

The Estate consists of Loseley House, some 1,400 acres, including 160 acres of woodland, the remainder divided between four farms and there are also fifty cottages. When I returned in 1946, few of the cottages were in good repair and only two or three had baths, WCs or electricity. Most cottages were rent-free, housing staff, the others let at not more than 5 shillings per week; all were built pre-1914, some in the sixteenth century. The Estate was responsible for the cost of maintenance.

For several years after taking over Loseley, I regarded the Estate as a millstone round my neck. There was the constant problem of maintenance backlog, it was loss-making and there were constant complaints. I could see a bright future for the farming with plenty of scope for expansion, the same with the concrete factory; but I resented the time I had to waste on unproductive Estate matters. Because there was no money for paying contractors to do repairs, we were dependent on Pop Reeve, the maintenance foreman, with his son Les and another assistant. Pop really knew all the rickety buildings, their weaknesses, their strengths and what he could get away with in terms of minimum input. He had become a wonderful 'bodger' and 'bodging' was the only option. Buildings were jacked up, shored and propped, leaks were plugged, cracks slurried over with cement, holes were filled, roofs patched. Tenants were long-suffering: there was no alternative and they must have realised that they were fortunate in paying such low rents.

In 1946 our tenant at Artington Manor Farm was John Brown, with his wife Mary. They took the Farm in 1923, moving down from Scotland straight from honeymoon. Very sadly, in 1950, John Brown died from a heart attack. I clearly remember his widow telephoning me the same day: 'I'm afraid it's bad news . . .' The son, Hugh, continued with the farming and his mother kept house until Hugh married Zoe a few years later. Mary Brown at 90 was on the Parish Council, and at 97 she is in fine fettle; as well as cooking and helping the family she is an active trustee of local charities.

Orange Court Farm in 1946 had a herd of Shorthorns, some arable and an acreage of vegetables. The tenant was another Scot, George Lyon, with his wife and two daughters. Tragically George was accidentally killed when jumping a ditch at the edge of a field with a shotgun, intending to attack the rooks on the emerging corn. This was the first farm to fall vacant. A hundred acres were taken in hand with the Home Farm and the remainder let to a young man, Gordon Palmer, married to Joan from New Zealand.

Binscombe Farm on the south end of the Estate was farmed by Percy Podger with his wife Ada, both from Dorset. The Podgers were sub-tenants, the Farm being let to F. R. Stovold Limited. Horses were the main interest and business of Percy and Ada, and their children Rosealee and Keith. There was a small dairy herd but the spread of housing development made this a difficult farm.

Mellersh Farm, some 200 acres, was occupied by Rex Marshall, a progressive farmer with his wife Phyllis, four sons and a daughter. There was a Friesian herd of cattle and, in the early days, vegetables and specialised crops were grown including opium poppies for production of oil used in paints, so we were told.

At Piccards we had Peter Glover and his lovely wife Sheila and eventually their six children. This 300-acre downland farm had a dairy herd and arable crops. Peter Glover was very active and, arriving at Loseley after war service as a Royal Marines officer, he expected instant action on repairs and any improvements he required, but we remained friends. Sadly, the farming did not prosper and eventually Peter left the Farm and went into other businesses. We took the Farm in hand, together with Mike Dancey, a real countryman, who was tractor driver and had worked on the Farm all his life.

Hard up though my parents were, they did not seem to bother about rents. This was partly because they regarded owning land as a privilege and they felt it wrong to profit from their tenants by charging what would be regarded as a fair rent. At that period rents generally were low, but ours were much lower than the normal and quite inadequate to maintain the properties, for which, in most cases, the Estate bore full liability. In 1946 our farms were let at £1 10 shillings (£1.50) per acre, including farmhouse, workers' cottages, farm buildings and land. The rent for 200-acre Mellersh Farm was around £300, which included three cottages and the farmhouse. Now owned by Mike, in 1995 the farmhouse alone is let for many times that figure, without the cottages, or the land and buildings, which Mike occupies with one of the Jersey herds.

My parents did not employ a firm of land agents on a regular basis but occasionally consulted a reliable local land agent and friend, Paul Luxmore-May. If a land agent had been employed on the Estate, he would have found it an unenviable assignment. He would have to report to the owners on the unacceptable condition of most of the buildings without being able to suggest how the necessary repairs could be funded. Any suggestion of increased rents would have been resented as much by the landowner as by the tenants.

Because of the lack of funds I did not employ an agent for some time and I personally dealt with all Estate matters, untrained and inexperienced though I was in the early days. Rents needed to go up and I started with Rex Marshall at Mellersh Farm. As already noted, he was getting a great deal for his £300 per annum. Rex had been kind and helpful to me in those early days, but, friend or not, £1 10s per acre was too low and I wrote to Rex proposing an increase to £2 10s per acre. The reply came not from Rex but from an estate agent acting on his behalf, contesting the increase. I was not prepared to negotiate with a professional, and if one side uses an agent, it is usual for the other party also to be professionally represented. I had met Mr Jim Eve MA FRICS, a land agent with an excellent reputation, a partner in Savills, and I asked him to act for me. To my amazement Rex was furious. We got our increased rent but sadly the relationship between Rex and myself never fully recovered and I never discovered why he was so upset. The low rents had been the policy for so long that Rex may have hoped that an agent's letter would procure a meek withdrawal: he did not know me very well. Rex and his family eventually emigrated to Australia and New Zealand and happily their farming 'Down Under' prospered. Rents on the other farms were increased without serious resistance.

I did not need an agent to make me aware of the poor condition of our cottages. We were not the only estate to have the problem of cottages requiring modernisation and a grant scheme was introduced offering grants of up to £400 per cottage for putting in baths and WCs and making other improvements. We took advantage of the grants and gradually got baths and WCs in all the cottages and did what we could to deal with rising damp and other problems. As the maintenance team already had an enormous workload, these improvements were put out to small builders.

After the first few years we had difficulty in recruiting good farm staff because of sub-standard cottages. 'I would like the job but the wife won't go into that house' was heard more than once. Understandably, they did not consider as idyllic a lovely, low-beamed sixteenth-century country cottage without electricity, that was cold and damp and smelling of mould, even though bath and WC had now been installed. To an estate agent the cottages *were* idyllic: one day I received an offer for four pairs of cottages in Littleton at £1,900 a pair. That sounds crazy today, especially as one converted pair was recently re-sold for some £400,000, but it did solve our problem. With the proceeds we erected three pairs of three-bedroomed cedar bungalows and a small flat, warm and well-appointed with Rayburn cookers, large kitchen/dining room and separate sitting room. These were manufactured by my firm Guildcrete. No more problems getting good staff and no maintenance. Also the appearance of the village was transformed, the new owners of the old cottages making them lovely outside as well as inside and creating beautiful gardens. Everyone was better off!

Another demand for capital expenditure arose for the Estate waterworks. The Estate has its own water supply: from earliest times this came from a spring at Conduit, on Piccards Farm at the bottom of the Downs. This spring still runs, the water now piped to the lake and the moat. From the early 1900s water was pumped from underground by an antiquated diesel-driven contraption to a large reservoir on the wooded ridge known as the East Warren, then flowing by gravity to the House, farms and most of the Estate. With the expansion of our livestock numbers, more water was needed and the old pump was getting unreliable: we had to spend money to put in a reliable system.

A friend, Sir Geoffrey Shakespeare, was a gifted water diviner. He located a spot near the main reservoir that he assured us would produce 5,000 gallons of water per hour. The geological survey executive put the rate at only 250 gallons per hour which would preclude us from grant aid. At the time BP were drilling for oil on the Estate – a 'dry well' it proved to be – and we persuaded them to drill a trial hole at Sir Geoffrey's chosen spot. Water engineer Colin Allsebrook's firm carried out pumping trials in the new bore and Sir Geoffrey's 5,000 gallons per hour was proved correct and we have never failed to obtain this yield. Allsebrooks designed a complex but most efficient pumping and control system with time clocks, pressure valves and sluices.

We also installed a 20 horsepower electric pump at the lake and an underground 4ins irrigation main running east/west across the Farm enabling us to irrigate the hundred acres of light soil on which early potatoes were grown in the rotation. The lake was also dredged, the first time this had been done mechanically. It would have been laborious with spades, wheelbarrows and planks.

We had a friend, Colin Bardwell, who lived at Compton where he was later Churchwarden. Colin was a partner in a local firm of estate agents, Weller Eggar, and I invited him to help me professionally in running the Estate and he readily agreed; this was one of my better decisions.

Colin is never in a hurry, always calm: appropriately he was soon appointed as a JP. When decisions had to be taken and the tenant was pressing for an answer, Colin would say quietly to me: 'We need not rush this, let it wait until our next meeting.' Afterwards he might add: 'The fellow will probably do it himself if we leave it.' Colin and I met for the best part of a day every eight weeks, reviewing the maintenance programme, tenancies, rents, insurances, requests for improvements, complaints, and we went and looked at items requiring attention and visited tenants. Loseley really meant something to Colin and his wife Betty. Thanks to Colin in the early 1970s we obtained a year-to-year tenancy of 500 acres on both sides of the Hog's Back and for six years we farmed a total of 1,500 acres – a rewarding but hectic experience!

Colin hated untidiness: 'He's a real mucker, that fellow' was a typical expression. We have not found anyone with the proverbial coal stored in the bath but one cottage inspection revealed a brood of chicks in the bath in one of the cottages!

When I inherited, I had heavy death duties to pay on the value of the House, its contents and the Estate. As there was no capital this sadly necessitated the sale of some property. For many years we have held a meeting in January, attended by Sue, Mike and I, Colin and our lawyer and accountant, to review the

position on potential death duties and to agree any action required
to reduce them to a minimum.

In the 1970s we obtained tax exemption for the House and contents, subject to their not being sold and, thanks to Colin's efforts,
the adjoining Heritage Land of 500 acres and twelve dwellings
were also exempted. For the time being I retained the exempt
properties and passed the remainder to Mike and to the Loseley
House Maintenance Fund (LHMF), which we had formed. The
LHMF Trust is administered by Trustees. Apart from avoiding
inheritance tax, the Trust also protects from a possible future
generation that 'backs slow horses and fast women'; we do not
forget that a wing of the House had to be pulled down in 1820
because of the extravagance of an earlier generation.

When thinking of financial matters there often comes into my
mind our Lord's injunction: 'Sell all that you have and give to
the poor.' Those words have often jolted my conscience. In fact,
I had virtually nothing of my own: Loseley was mortgaged and we
were overdrawn at the bank. Of course I could have sold the lot
and would have had quite a bit left after paying off the mortgage
and overdraft, but I held Loseley in trust for future generations.
One is merely steward for life and not in a position to sell. I
also wanted Loseley to be put to good use and no one can say
that we are keeping it to ourselves, with over 100,000 people a
year coming here; even more important and satisfying to Sue
and me is the Christian Centre.

So, I have not sold and given to the poor. I do not feel entirely
free from guilt, but one of the better things that I have done
was setting up our Charitable Trusts: the Loseley and Guildway
Charitable Trust, mainly for compassionate causes, and the Loseley
Christian Trust, for Christian causes, with priority for the healing
ministry and evangelism. At the time we had no funds to put in, so
borrowed from the bank to get them started. I then transferred five
cottages to the Charitable Trust and later two cottages in Littleton
and the Estate Church of St Francis Littleton to the Christian Trust.
I gave 40 per cent of my Guildway shareholding to the Trusts and
30 per cent of my Loseley Dairy Products shares; and Sue and
Mike also gave a considerable proportion of their shares. When
first Guildway and then Loseley Dairy Products were sold it was
very satisfying that the Trusts were relatively well funded and had
no tax to pay. A Vodafone aerial site was also gifted to the Christian

Trust, for which it provides a rent of £3,500 per annum and looks less hideous when considered as 'a beacon for Christ'!

The formation of the two Charitable Trusts has tied up funds and properties that would otherwise be available for Loseley's owners, but we must be prepared to help others in need, and there are so many. The Trusts enable the family to give to compassionate and Christian causes without having to make difficult decisions on what they personally can afford, and I hope that in years to come more owners will set up genuine Charitable Trusts.

Colin retired in 1988, having sold, with his partners, the firm Weller Eggar to the Leeds Building Society. I needed someone like Colin, who would have a feel for Loseley and be interested and involved. We saw one or two people and then Nigel Draffan, Nigel Clutton and Mike Mills of Cluttons Arundel Office came round and I knew that we had found the right people. A year or so later Nigel received well-deserved promotion at Goodwood but is still involved with Loseley rather more than his 'watching brief' infers.

One day Sue and I, when visiting Cluttons Offices at Arundel, met a bright young trainee, Tim Butler; we felt sure that he would do well. Two years later Cluttons proposed that we set up an accounting system for all Loseley properties, using Cluttons' computer. This had been operated very successfully at another estate managed by Cluttons, through young Tim Butler from Arundel. A meeting was held at Loseley to discuss this. There was some opposition to the proposal but the simplicity and clarity of the scheme coupled with the dramatic improvement on the other estate were compelling and I pressed for agreement. We took on Tim and the system and in the first year our Estate accounts were transformed and we were profitable; the second year was better still. Tim pays weekly visits and we have a quarterly meeting attended also by Nigel, Colin as Trustee, Mike and myself. Coopers, Reading were the accountants working with Cluttons on the other estate, with Bob Harland doing the taxation advisory work, so we took them on as well.

The Estate is, I believe, well managed despite its complexity. For many years I had been the sole owner, which made for simplicity. Now, to save inheritance tax, the Estate is divided between Mike, the Maintenance Fund, the Charitable Trusts and one house to Sue with the exempt property still in my name: complex, but the computer does not seem to mind. Mike, having taken over the farming and business side now plays the major role on the Estate.

We have always enjoyed a good relationship with our local authority. Under reorganisation in 1974, the RDC merged with Guildford Borough and to mark the occasion, coinciding with my year as High Sheriff of Surrey, we donated the Lordship of the Manor of Compton Common at a special ceremony to the new Borough of Guildford. The Common is unspoilt, as a natural habitat, under the ever-watchful eye of Mrs Kathleen McAlmont and the Elizabeth McAlmont Memorial Trust. I remember my father saying: 'We've got splendid Chief Officers in the RDC.' This still applies to the Borough Council with David Watts, Chief Executive, and John Nightingale, Chief Planning Officer, among others. We maintain close liaison and we trust one another. Mike has been developing further our links with the Council, and at their suggestion we held a series of meetings with the Planning department to draw up a 'Loseley Estate Management Plan'. This includes access, traffic, planning, environment, nature trails, woodlands, farming, alternative use of buildings, the visiting public, signs. The officers understand the importance of the Estate being profitable.

The environment is important. Loseley is a place of great beauty, to be experienced rather than described. The mellowness of the House, ancient stone from Waverley Abbey, backdrop to velvet lawns, the Park with its oak trees, the fields sloping down to the pond in the valley. Ducks and moorhens on the water, sometimes reflections of cows that are grazing adjoining fields. Then the upward slope of the sandy land, where early potatoes grew. At the top of the ridge the East and West Warren woods, home to rabbits still. The woods link the family generations, each harvesting trees planted by great-great-grandparents and beyond, and planting for generations unborn. The Loseley woods are of mixed species and uneven aged, planned for amenity. Each wood has its own character and atmosphere: the lighter, elegant firs and sycamores of the sandy Warrens, the great oaks, solid and dignified, on the heavier land. Spring after spring, very special to me, are the primroses, bluebells and wild orchids of Ashen Copse. Much more could be written about the woods but a quotation from our eminent friend, the late Sir Ronald Harris must suffice:

He that planteth a tree is a servant of God.
He provideth a kindness for many generations
And faces that he has not seen shall bless him.

We have already paid tribute to Pop Reeve, the master bodger. When Pop retired Fred Gooch took over, as narrated earlier. Although Fred was active with the sawmill, making products and erecting new buildings on the Farm, the maintenance of buildings was not neglected. We were beginning to catch up but it would be many years before one could say that all was in good order. Within two years Fred had to transfer full-time to manufacturing houses at the Artington factory and he handed over as maintenance foreman to Pop's son Les. Les, after leaving the army with the rank of sergeant, had been working under Pop in the maintenance team. Able and conscientious, Les was also particularly kind and helpful. Very sadly, he suffered from lung trouble and died shortly before he was due for retirement.

Les was followed by another ex-Queens Regiment sergeant, Larry Sheppard. Larry had done some improvement jobs on Loseley cottages as a self-employed builder and we got on well together. Larry was a practical person and liked to see the whole job through, including the plumbing and wiring if he got the chance.

Among permanent reminders of Larry is the full-size cross that he made for the Pilgrimage Staircase from 350-year-old oak, and the smaller cross in the Chapel. Larry played an important part in the erection of the Tithe Barn and, with Fred, the laying of its 2,000 sq. ft oak floor. Larry retired in 1985 but he still helps in an emergency. As I write, last Sunday the water supply failed. Mike and family were away skiing. Cowman from Mellersh Farm at the door: 'Cows have no water.' I ring Alan, the maintenance foreman. Daughter answers: 'Sorry they're away for the day.' Ring Larry. For a long time no answer, then a very weak voice croaks: 'Hello.' Larry is in bed with flu but asserts that he'll come up. Met him at the pump house, looking very rough. 'It's them fuses again. Be all right now.' It's people like Larry that keep alive the Co-Partnership's spirit.

Larry could tackle all the maintenance jobs, including the water supply, but for Fred Gooch, in his day, this was not enough; he wanted to make products for sale.

CHAPTER 6

TO THE BRINK

Fred Gooch joined us in 1953, Coronation year. 'Let's make flag poles for sale to retired naval officers,' proposed Fred. He cut poles from the woods, stripped the bark, attached the cleats and other accessories, did the painting, and Fred and Les delivered and erected on Saturdays. Fred then made up chicken coops and crates and sold them in Guildford market on Tuesdays. Farmers in the market enquired about sheds and poultry houses; Fred did a rough sketch on the back of an envelope, worked out the price and took the order. At first these products were produced by the maintenance department in evening overtime, after the day's work on the backlog of building repairs. Soon we had built up a range of timber buildings and poultry equipment to complement the Guildcrete concrete buildings and pig troughs. We advertised in the farming press and then had to increase the staff to keep up with demand.

Fred and I met every Wednesday morning at 7.00am in the Farm Office to plan the work programme, discuss marketing and ordering of materials. Occasionally Fred would tentatively suggest spending £100 or so – a big sum for us – on a secondhand machine. This was a very satisfying period; our discussions were always open and harmonious: Fred and I respected one another and we dedicated ourselves to building up the business. Fred knew the technicalities and I made the policy and financial decisions; we very seldom disagreed and never argued.

One day Fred mentioned that there was no reason why we should not make timber dwelling houses. It seemed an interesting idea for the longer-term future. Soon afterwards, in October 1954, on holiday in Scotland, Sue and I spent a night in Edinburgh. In the hotel that evening I remembered that there was a firm called Crudens near Edinburgh making timber houses. Next morning I telephoned Crudens; the Chairman, Harry Cruden, was in his office and said he would be pleased to see us and take us round the show bungalow. The bungalow was delightful, clad in Canadian red cedar – free from rot and insect attack, as Mr Cruden emphasised.

We liked Harry Cruden, who gave us permission to manufacture the bungalows in England, and in return we agreed to allow Crudens to manufacture our farm buildings in Scotland. We were travelling northwards and arranged to call again a few days later. We returned home with the manufacturing rights for southern England. Fred was thrilled and still has the letter I wrote from Oban, dated 11th October 1954, informing him about the Crudens cedar bungalows. Not long afterwards Crudens, who had wide interests in construction, bricks, joinery and steel fabrication, dropped the bungalow production and allowed us to sell anywhere.

By that time I had learned the hard way a good deal about business and manufacturing, but little did we realise the implications of what we were taking on with manufacturing houses. From the production aspect there are not too many problems in moving from farm buildings to houses, but in financing, administration, purchasing, complexity of control and marketing, undercover storage requirements, there is a world of difference. There were additional problems, including obtaining planning consents: in those days there was prejudice against timber housing and the bad image of the immediate post-war 'Pre-fabs' did not help.

No sane person in our situation and without capital would have gone ahead. We were full of enthusiasm and optimism and from the start this permeated us all, providing the momentum we needed. Fred soon had the first cedar bungalow in production, to the Cruden design, complete with the reeded cedar cladding. By a happy coincidence at that time a Guildford Ideal Homes Exhibition was staged for ten days alongside the A3, and our cedar bungalow was the only house erected at that Exhibition. Over 30,000 people visited the house. We were ecstatic, but thousands of people through a show house and enthusiastic comments do not amount to orders. Apart from the problems in getting planning consent, nearly all our prospective clients had to find and purchase land on which to build the house. Many potential customers were unable to proceed because they could not find a suitable plot or obtain planning consent or satisfactory mortgage.

At the end of the Exhibition we took the house down and transported it to a Loseley site at Down Lane, Compton, re-erected and rented it to our accountant. This was to be the first show house of many in later years to be taken down after an Exhibition and re-erected, including a number from the *Daily Mail* Ideal Home Exhibition at Olympia, where we exhibited for many years, and houses at overseas exhibitions in Paris, Lyons, Hamburg, Stuttgart, Amsterdam and Italy. Some European housing exhibitions were laid out as model villages and the houses remained on site for sale as residences.

From the beginning we were determined to set a high standard of quality in materials, workmanship and service right down to the small details, and we never deviated from this policy. Our Canadian structural timber was surfaced four sides (planed) for precision construction. After the first year all structural timbers were pressure-treated against rot and insect attack: not many houses then had treated timbers. The western red cedar cladding contains natural oils which provide the necessary deterrent. Quality, service and integrity were fundamental to our business and this was instilled into all our members, including builders and clients, from the start. We never relaxed this policy, building a sound reputation for reliability which was remarked on by many of our customers; one overseas customer stated that he would trust us more than a company in his own country. Another oft-repeated comment by visitors to the factory, including those from overseas, was on the friendly atmosphere. Certainly we could have been more profitable and 'successful' if we had striven ruthlessly for profit above all else but I make no apology for stressing our policy for high standards and putting people before maximum profit.

Having said that, I admit that we needed to be really profitable and we were very under-capitalised. Virtually inexperienced, we were among the pioneers of a new industry manufacturing houses, with a notoriously high percentage of business failures. During my thirty-seven years as Chairman, finance was always the biggest problem. The £20,000 overdraft was to creep up to £1,600,000, but that was many years ahead.

1955 was an eventful year, starting up the production and marketing of the bungalows and battling for planning consents and mortgages, finding plots and good builders. We formed Loseley Construction to erect the bungalows and farm buildings, and after making the panels for the early bungalows in the Estate yard we moved production to the Guildcrete site at the bottom of the drive. We made twenty bungalows that year, in addition to an enlarged range of concrete and timber farm buildings. One of the earliest orders was for a well-known local architect for his own occupation, John Brownrigg ARIBA, who was also to become consultant architect to the firm and a valuable member of the team. After erecting the first two bungalows with our own staff, we realised that it was not practical to take responsibility for erection all over the country and we decided to work through reliable local builders, who were encouraged to regard themselves as part of our team. Choosing the right builder was vital: our reputation was staked on their workmanship.

In 1956 we held our first Builders Day for erectors and prospective erectors of our bungalows and farm buildings. It was a friendly and informal gathering at the Jolly Farmer Inn attended by some half dozen small builders from Surrey, Sussex and Berkshire, together with Fred and myself and our construction manager. Some forty years on, two of these family firms, Strong Brothers of Caversham and Vinalls of Henfield, are still regularly building Guildway houses. Builders Days were to become a regular and important feature of our business; later named Builders Conventions and attended by up to three hundred delegates, we later progressed from the Jolly Farmer to the Park Lane Hilton, the Guildford Civic Hall and to our Artington headquarters.

We always emphasised the importance of people and of teamwork. We referred to our Convention guests as 'members of the Guildway Club', regarding as friends everyone involved in our business – employees, builders, distributors, bankers, suppliers, professional advisers, building societies. 'We are mutually dependent,' I always reminded them. If the builder does a bad job in erecting a house it damages our reputation, and if we fail to deliver on time, the builder is held up. Within the firm I frequently reminded our people that each one of us played an important part in our success. If the receptionist was slow in answering the telephone or treated a caller in an offhand fashion, she could damage our reputation and lose a customer; in fact, our receptionists did an excellent job in creating a helpful image. Fred was an extrovert and made friends with builders, suppliers and everyone with whom we did business. If someone could not get on with Fred there was something wrong with them!

As the firm developed and grew my workload as Managing Director increased, but I also continued for many years to run the expanding farming operations at Loseley and the Estate still demanded some of my time. Thanks to Sue's hard work and dedication in restoring the main wing at Loseley, the House was now open to the public. In all directions, tremendous activity, much to show for it, but no money: crisis!

Guildcrete, due to all the activity in introducing the bungalows, had plunged into a big loss in 1955 and the financial situation was rapidly worsening in the early months of 1956. Our original financial adviser and auditor, a charming fellow, appeared out of his depth: 'You always try to run before you can walk' was true enough, but no help to us or our creditors. Our friend and family solicitor, Meryn Lewis, then recommended Gilbert Potier.

Gillie, as he was known, was a brilliant accountant, partner in a City firm and a company director. Aged about 40 at the time, he was destined to become managing director and then chairman of Consolidated Goldfields. An RAF pilot in the war, DFC and Bar, Gillie was alert, dark and athletic, an excellent hockey, tennis and squash player with a very quick eye. Perfectionist and meticulous almost to a fault, Gillie had his hair cut every week at Harrods; always correct in his dress as in all things, he kept two hats in his car. The trilby was exchanged for the bowler on the A3 at Putney Vale; Sue and I actually witnessed this change of headgear one evening, going to London with him.

Gillie soon had a clear grasp of our company and its problems and came down for half a day a fortnight to help to get the situation under control. He and I used to go through the list of creditors and debtors, deciding what could be done to stave off the creditors and how to put further pressure on the debtors. We banned any expenditure not absolutely essential. In between Gillie's visits, I contacted the chief executives or financial officers of all our main suppliers and explained the position, asked for a little more time, told them when we expected to be able to pay, subsequently always informing them if this date could not be met. I always offered to visit personally for talks if required. We had built up a good relationship with our suppliers and let them know how important they were to us, how we valued their support. All except one of our suppliers trusted me and gave us up to five months credit, even though aware of our perilous situation. These loyal suppliers included John Foot and Nevil Chamberlain of Angel, Son and Gray, Raymond Moon of John Moon and Son, Farquharson and Daniels, both large timber suppliers. The loyalty of these firms was not forgotten, friendships deepened and we continued to trade with those who supported us for many years to come and in much greater volume. The exception was the merchant who supplied our cement. I had called on the chairman and explained the situation and agreed a credit limit. Soon afterwards, without warning, the weekly delivery failed to appear and production of concrete products came to a halt. We switched to direct supply by the cement manufacturer and saved 2½ per cent on the price.

Underpinning my efforts for survival was my faith in God and prayer. Not pleading for money to flow in, not praying for profitability but for strength and discernment. For as long as I can remember I have prayed daily: prayer becomes part of one's ongoing relationship with God. Thanksgiving is as significant as prayer for help.

I was doing everything possible to raise further funds: meetings with the bank manager to reassure him, visiting the NFU Insurance Society at Stratford on Avon to increase the mortgage on Loseley, offering large discounts for customers prepared to pay in advance and finally asking four personal friends for unsecured loans at 10 per cent interest. One, a wealthy property developer, turned me down flat with a joke about learning the hard way. Two, John Dixey and Rennie and Donny were absolutely splendid and immediately agreed to put up £2,000 each without any quibbles.

The fourth was an elderly couple that I did not know well; I had not asked them for a loan but queried whether they felt I might approach their nephew, who lived on his agricultural estate in Scotland. They indicated that he was involved in a lot of capital expenditure on his estate and probably an approach would not be appropriate at this stage. I quite understood, thanked them and apologised and we parted amicably. Next day a £2,000 cheque arrived from the couple with a note: 'Hope this will prove a catch penny. With best wishes . . .' Six months later I was able to repay the first instalment of £1,000. I received a note in response: 'Your cheque burns beautifully.' The £2,000 which that wonderful couple gave me was to be of lasting significance. Not only did it play an important part in getting through our crisis but it set me an example and in the years to come I was able to help a number of people who were in financial need, saying that it was money that had been given to me. That gift, and more, has now been re-used many times over in helping others. I hope that my elderly friends got as much satisfaction from the original gift to me as I have had in passing it on. I still remember them every week.

By May 1956 the auditors had decided that liquidation of the company was inevitable. A liquidation statement was prepared: creditors would not receive more than half a crown (12½p) in the pound. On 23rd May I travelled to London to be briefed by Gillie on the procedure for liquidation. On the train I went through the list of creditors yet again. Surely Raymond Moon would give me another two weeks – and Angel, Son and Gray . . . and William Evans . . . they trust me, and the orders *will* come. No accountant, no hard-headed businessman would have gone along with this for a moment. The situation was hopeless and the auditors, even Gillie, had said so.

I arrived a few minutes early at the offices of Limebeer and Company, Chartered Accountants, at 2 Broadstreet Place. The lift was antiquated, the manually operated latticed metal doors clanged uncertainly and I was conveyed slowly upwards to the fourth floor. The receptionist ushered me along the gloomy corridor to the Board Room to await Mr Potier. It was a sombre room, long and rather narrow, dark brown the prevailing colour – the long polished table, flanked by brown leather chairs, dark wooden bookcases, containing row upon row of legal and accountancy tomes lined the side walls. I made my way to the window at the far end of the room.

It was a warm sunny day and one of the sash windows was open. Looking down from the fourth floor I was aware, as in a dream, of taxis and cars coming and going in the street below. Men walking, several in bowler hats, coming and going . . . Why did they bother to come or to go, hither or thither – what was the point? There was no point to my existence any more. My little world had crashed. All I had worked for, hoped for . . . My dreams – all washed up, finished. All those who had trusted me with credit, with money, those who had stood by me, had been reassured by me – no, misled – I had let them all down. And our loyal employees. My world had crashed.

If you saw that wonderful film *Love Story* in the mid-1970s, you may remember the scene where the young principal character, having been told that his wife is dying, walks aimlessly down the road. The atmosphere of desolation and helplessness is enhanced by the music. As, years later, I watched that scene in the film it mirrored completely my feelings of desolation at that window some twenty years before. I thought of those men who had jumped out of skyscraper windows in the American Depression of the 1930s: I could absolutely understand why they did it – the feelings of disgrace, despair. I had no thought at jumping myself, that would be pointless.

At that moment my musings were interrupted by the arrival of Gillie Potier. His usual warm and friendly greeting was muted and we were both too aware of the gravity of the occasion for any small talk. He was, I knew, about to announce the death sentence on my company. I found myself forestalling him: 'Gillie, I am not going to liquidate.'

'James, you have got to face the facts. Your company is insolvent. You are aware of this, so you personally are liable for any debts that the company cannot meet; you have no money, so you are putting Loseley at risk. Your major creditors are owed at least four months, some five months, and there is no hope of getting more from them. You are right up to your overdraft limit and the bank has stated that they will not give you any more. You are not trading profitably and you are short of orders. It is very sad, but you have to face the facts. You cannot survive.'

'I am not going to liquidate.'

'Well, if that's your firm decision, good luck to you, James.'

Gillie and I went on to dine with our mutual friend and lawyer, Meryn Lewis, and his wife Gwen at their house in Kensington, where our wives also met up with us. Meryn was almost as dedicated to Loseley's survival as were Sue and myself. I was apprehensive of Meryn's reaction to learning of my stubborn refusal to liquidate. Everyone was incredulous when on our arrival Gillie announced: 'James is not going to liquidate.' The tenseness fell from Meryn's face. Smiling, he said: 'I shall really enjoy my dinner after all' – and so did we all.

Early next morning I told Fred that we were not liquidating. He too was absolutely thrilled – though none of us had any idea as to how we could survive. I just knew we would: perhaps just a question of faith. The first thing Fred and I did was to drive to Alan Potter's house in Farncombe. Alan had been our only technician/designer, a quiet shy person in his early 30s, very conscientious and reliable. Sadly we had had to dispense with his services two weeks before because we could not afford even his modest salary. But without a technician there was no future and as we were continuing in business we needed him. Alan came to the door, somewhat surprised to see us. 'Alan, have you found a job?' A rather embarrassed and hesitant admission that so far there was nothing definite. 'Alan, will you come back?' We took him on immediately, with rejoicing.

The very next week orders started to pick up. There was no particular reason for this, but it was very significant. Although still showing a loss, we had record sales in the second half-year. New farm building lines were also introduced, the most successful being the Silo Barn, benefiting from the newly introduced silo grant. The next year Fred Gooch received his well-earned promotion to the Board as technical director. Fred and I felt certain that our future growth lay in housing and we formed a new company, Cedar Homes Limited, for the bungalows.

No one ever suggested liquidation to me again, although we were seldom far from the brink, with deep financial problems over the next quarter century. The effects on my life of the company's survival were to be more dramatic and significant than I could have imagined. I did not have long to wait.

Miss Nancy Bulbeck and Miss Ann Bardley, bottling milk,
Loseley Dairy, 1923.

Rosie Hunter, John Webber and supervisor Steve Pudney with Ampac
machine, potting yoghourt, Loseley Dairy, 1995.

My father, 'The General', on his mare Ivylass with top model Barbara Goalen at the first photographic modelling session at Loseley, *c.*1950.

Our wedding day, October 1948. Compton Church path under an archway of pitchforks and hoes held by Farm and Estate staff.

Cathedral Grove, Vancouver Island, 1971. Mick English and myself, co-founders in 1947 of Guildcrete Ltd.

Sue ploughing Front Park with the Ferguson tractor, 1950.

Farm Co-Partnership meeting, 1951. *From left to right:* my father,
myself, Miss Bennett, Bert Griffin, Richard Atkin, Tom Enticknap,
Colin Reeve, Tom Reeve, Fred Nash, Tom Winser.

Farm Co-Partnership meeting, *c*.1980. *From left to right:* Daphne
Holloway, David Cripps, James Walters, myself, Sue, Tom Reeve, Tom
Enticknap, Fred Nash, Les Reeve.

Hon Chaplain Canon Hudson at staff party 1974, with John and Christine West.

Guildway Board at Loseley. *From left to right:* Stephen Davies, Fred Gooch, Bill Harris, David Kane, Brian Hall, Meryn Lewis, myself.

Guildway factory and trailers ready for shipment to Nigeria.

Guildway housing production line. Computerised frame-making machine in foreground, operator Geoff Mitchell.

Mike and Sarah.

Our grandchildren.
From left to right: Tristram, Katrina, Alexander, Christopher.

Dr Chris Jagger, Sue, myself and the Revd Pat Ashe, founders of
Loseley Christian Cancer Help Centre.

At the top of the Staircase Pilgrimage: the Cross and, through the
doorway, the Chapel.

Loseley Organic Bakery. The cheerful Stephen Cheeseman, baker and champion ploughman, with Liz Coote, whose father and grandfather also worked on the Estate, and Hazel Marks.

Long service members, 1974. *Standing:* Richard, herdsman; Les, maintenance; Fred Gooch; Fred, stockman; Fred, woodman; Tom, garden manager. *Seated:* Tom, retired; Tom, tractor driver/garden.

CHAPTER 7

TO HIGHER THINGS

One evening at the Provost of Guildford's Industry Discussion Group we had a talk from the late Sir Alfred Owen, a dedicated Christian and Chairman of Rubery Owen, then the largest private company in the UK. Sir Alfred told of giving his Christian testimony at his 21st birthday party. 'Nail your colours to the mast,' he urged.

It had been instilled into me that one should not talk religion in public, but Sir Alfred impressed me. If the opportunity should come I resolved to follow his example and I did not have long to wait. In the period since the 'non-liquidation', less than two years, the company had expanded. To provide more offices we built an upper floor extension.

On St Valentine's Day 1958 Sue and I arranged for the opening of the new Guildcrete offices to be carried out by our Rector at Compton, Canon Aelfric Hudson. Kind and friendly, Canon Hudson was tall and heavily built with a deep booming voice. He had a pronounced limp, wounded by a shell in the First World War which killed the five soldiers with him. Aelfric hated pomposity and if anyone considered himself important he would say: 'Let's award him Oxo with cubes.' He loved God and he loved people and remembered their names and their children's names. I had arranged with the Canon that he would also take on the appointment of Honorary Chaplain to the company. He was the ideal person, going round the factory and offices, talking to people, sensitively knowing when a person was too busy to talk or occasionally those who did not want to be seen with him. Many were helped by his friendship and wisdom. There are always tensions when the subject of religion is raised: it is 'a personal matter' and the Chaplain needs to go unaccompanied; he certainly must not be accompanied by the Chairman!

In introducing Canon Hudson on that Valentine's Day I told the assembled company why I had chosen a Minister of Religion to open our new offices: this was an act of thanksgiving to God. We had come through a very difficult period: the experts had said that we could not survive and without my faith in God we would have gone into liquidation. It is lonely at the top, tough decisions have to be taken and I had been strengthened through prayer. I then invited Aelfric to open the offices, and he gave a splendid address on the dignity of work:

> By what goes out from here men and women will be blessed . . . You will be rewarded by the satisfaction that grows with reputation, of straight dealing, good craftsmanship, honest achievement. The satisfaction that through your work you have made good houses that can be made into happy homes. We owe a duty to God and a duty to our fellow men. And by its fulfilment we do discover, little by little, the meaning of happiness for ourselves and blessing for all who come into contact with us and our handiwork. I want you all to feel something of what our Lord does impress upon us . . . and that is the dignity, the honour and the potential for happiness in our work.

Perhaps the most significant aspect of that day was that I had 'nailed my colours to the mast'. Nothing would be quite the same again and God was to respond unexpectedly and more deeply and powerfully than I could have imagined.

The next year, 1959, saw considerable increase in turnover which brought us back at last into profit. Fred and I had been reading about the Manufactured Housing Industry in the USA. There were several companies manufacturing homes, covering between them all the States of the USA. We became members of the American Home Manufacturers Association and we received visits from executives of US Home Manufacturing companies. We learned from these people, and the most interesting news was that brick skins were now being applied to timber-frame manufactured homes. Previously the panels had been clad with wood boarding, as our cedar bungalows. With the new system, the structural panels formed load-bearing walls and provided the insulation; the roof could be erected immediately the panels were fixed in position, after which the outside skin of brick or local stone is erected, so that the house blends in with its surroundings. This was really exciting, for most of our problems over planning consents would be overcome and the brick skin also opened up the town housing market: cedar cladding restricted us to spacious rural sites.

Fred is a tremendous enthusiast but I have seldom seen him so thrilled as when I told him I proposed booking us in for the Home Manufacturers Association Convention at Roanoake, Virginia, in October 1959. We agreed to visit as many Home Manufacturing firms as possible to study production, sales, transport and all aspects. We also had some farm building projects to research, including advanced poultry equipment and tower silos. We received several invitations from Home Manufacturers and universities in Virginia, Maryland, Ohio, Indiana, as well as the Washington DC headquarters of HMA, and also from Toronto where we visited the famous Agricultural Fair. Always short of money, we were concerned at the cost of the airfare. We went by BOAC Britannia, a fifteen-hour flight during which I sat next to an American lady who spent the night writing interminable letters copied straight out of a number of guidebooks.

Arrived at the airport, now known as JFK, we at once ran into language problems and the officials were unfriendly to the point of rudeness. The area surrounding ports and airports in most countries is often depressingly ugly but the journey from the airport to New York was particularly awful, the landscape desecrated by haphazard unsightly buildings, ugly iron bridges and enormous advertising hoardings exhorting one, among other things, to 'Chew Burmah tobacco'. A roadside sign which I did not find objectionable: 'Keep right with God'.

We were tired after the fifteen-hour flight without sleep. We had suffered rudeness at the airport and what we had seen of the surroundings on the journey to New York did nothing to raise our spirits. We lunched in a modest restaurant; iced water was instantly produced without our asking and courteous and very quick service restored our morale. At the Convention Hotel in Roanoake, Virginia, a little black waitress was intrigued: she had never seen an Englishman before. Peering at us with her great shining eyes, shyly she asked: 'You English? Say somepin.' 'Yes we are. Glad to meet you.' Our response was greeted with an embarrassed fit of giggles. A hundred years earlier she might well have been a slave. In the South, the Civil War was still very much a talking point and people wanted to show us battlefields. Some of the parents of our American friends had been involved in that terrible war.

At the three-day Convention we met the top people from the main Home Manufacturers in the USA and Canada. Everyone was friendly, on Christian name terms and very helpful. Nearly all invited us to visit their plants: we accepted as many as possible and received wonderful hospitality. The first thing we noticed outside factories was an enormous car park full of cars. 'Whose cars?' we asked. 'The guys in the plant' was the somewhat astonished reply. We were amazed: this was 1959 and our workers in the factory came by bike and bus and all we had to provide were cycle stands. Before long we too had to provide a large car park.

Our hosts answered all our questions, showed us everything we wanted to see, sometimes mentioning that they would not show that particular item to an American competitor. They gave us costings, demonstrated techniques and machines, put us in touch with suppliers. There is more enthusiasm evident than in England, and even the wives of senior executives tend to know about the technical details of housing. At dinner one evening our hostess replied to my question that, of course, she knew the width of a standard door. Making houses was her husband's profession and she had to be well-versed in it and to be able to give him her full support. Wives were more up-front than at home and expected to be involved in business entertaining.

Mostly we stayed in motels – cheap, clean and convenient – as we journeyed in our Hertz Chevvy. After taking us round their factories and offices our succession of hosts would take us home for a meal. In probably half the houses we visited, Grace was said before meals and our hosts were keen to talk about their church and their Christian faith and work. Everywhere we went there seemed to be a new church being built by some denomination; apparently nearly all these buildings are paid for by their congregations and the minister is also dependent on the congregation for his salary, normally well above UK stipends. I visited the Franciscan Friary in New York and when we had time to spare I would visit the Roman Catholic church of the locality, appreciating the prayerful and devotional atmosphere.

Arriving at our Indianapolis motel, I was thrilled to see on the neon welcome sign 'Billy Graham'! Unknown to us, he was speaking at Indianapolis Stadium that evening. I was one of the last to arrive at the packed Stadium and had to go right to the top to get a seat. At the end of his inspiring talk, Billy Graham assured us that we were all saved but that anyone who had any doubt about their personal salvation should come forward. I certainly did not feel that I could claim: 'I am saved', so I got out of my seat for the long and embarrassing walk to the Arena, aware of thousands of eyes upon me and very few others coming forward. The music became soft as Billy Graham asked everyone to pray for those coming forward. 'However great their sins, God will forgive them. Pray . . . Quietly pray.' Still very few had moved from their seats and I felt very self-conscious wearing, I remember, my very English mackintosh.

Our American journey came less than eighteen months after a deep experience of God and I had a great hunger for spirituality. This in no way diminished the intensity of my interest in the Home Manufacturing Industry that we had come to see: the two were linked. We went round plant after plant, asking questions, taking notes and photographs – machines we had never heard of or imagined: truss presses, component cutters, door hanging machines, conveyor systems, mechanical loaders, self feeders. Fred got a rapid grasp of technical details and manufacturing techniques. I concentrated on new ideas, marketing, policy, organisation. We visited show houses, learned about company mortgage lending schemes and support for builders and developers. As well as all the help and hospitality received from the Home Manufacturers, we had a warm reception from universities in Pennsylvania, Virginia and Maryland. Professors and staff were allocated to us to provide information on subjects that interested us, and then we would be taken to farms to see practical examples of these and other items of interest. These visits usually included our receiving hospitality in the home of the person taking us round. I doubt if an American equipment manufacturer would receive anything approaching the facilities or the hospitality showered on us in the USA.

We had seen so much and had accumulated piles of brochures, plans, details, samples, tape recordings, notes. So many factories, all these new machines, new ideas, new techniques, new marketing strategies. I clearly remember, near the end of our last week, saying to Fred: 'There are two vital things which, on their own, make this tour pay off – we must put a brick skin on our houses and we must sell to developers and builders and not to individuals', as we were doing at that time. Fred agreed and we put these concepts into effect immediately we got back. The team at Artington responded with enthusiasm.

In retrospect this was the most dynamic, exciting and worthwhile period in our history. We were pioneering a new industry in the UK, possibly first also in Europe. Our colleagues were eager to hear all our news. Reports were typed and circulated, talks given, questions answered and slides viewed. A local engineering firm was briefed by Fred and given details for manufacturing a door hanging machine and another firm was briefed to make a truss press and plates, the first machine of its kind in Europe.

On the design side, within a week of our return, Alan Potter – thankfully re-recruited the day after the 'non-liquidation' – had produced plans of a brick skin America-line bungalow which was manufactured and erected within a few weeks of our return. Alan bought this package from the firm and had it erected for his own occupation in 1960: it is still his lovely home in 1995. Now commonplace, this was the very first manufactured timber-frame brick skin dwelling ever erected in the United Kingdom.

There was so much enthusiasm in the firm at all levels – the Board, factory, office staff. We were a real team and we worked fast. No computers in those days; we made decisions and got on with it. It is worth recording that Fred and I returned from America in early December 1959, and five months later, in May 1960, we launched the America-line range of brick skin timber-frame houses to the Press and representatives of the building industry at the Conaught Rooms, London. In less than six months the America-line house had been designed by Alan Potter, with some final detailing by our consultant architect, John Brownrigg, the first house had been manufactured and erected on Alan's plot, we had produced cost and erection instructions, plans and brochures, advertisements – everything required for the public launch of a system of construction never previously seen in the UK. Despite the short timescale, all details were correct and the house, plans and the literature were of good quality.

Years later, when the firm had grown and we had computers, computer-controlled machines and other complex devices, when I asked the technical department for some minor changes to a house design, I was usually told that this would be very difficult and would take a long time because it was not on the computer programme. How one hankered for those early days when things were simple; we had few people but so much enthusiasm! Much of the credit for the speed of these operations must go to Fred, who at that time was both Sales Manager and Technical Director. Fred had ensured that the sales force assisted in erecting the first house.

As we expected, the brick skin greatly widened our market, and selling to builders and developers boosted sales and streamlined marketing. Selling to builders and developers could result in orders from the client for hundreds of houses over a year or two, whereas selling to private clients produced, at best, one house ordered and often much abortive work. As anticipated, these two new introductions transformed the business.

1961 saw the full benefit of the new changes and sales increased by over 100 per cent to 160 houses. Then in 1962 to 235, 1963 to 379, rising to 915 houses in 1967 and 1,175 in 1973. It became clear that we were on to a winner. We had to concentrate all our efforts on the housing and reluctantly we ceased production of concrete products, including blocks which started us off in business, and of farm buildings, which we had claimed to be the widest range in the country.

Our first exports were to Germany. Fred and I had made an exploratory visit in 1962 and appointed a distributor, the following year forming our own subsidiary company, Guildway (Deutschland) GmbH, based in Hamburg. This did not prove to be one of our best ideas. Being short of capital, we had to do things on a shoestring and we discovered that Germans tend to mistrust small firms and small adverts, and with only classified ads we made slow progress. There are problems in controlling operations in a foreign country and a great deal of extra work is involved. All sales literature had to be translated into German and technical details altered to comply with stringent German regulations, which were very precise and subject to minor variations in the different States (Länder). Our first Geschäftsführer (General Manager) was very industrious but not very bright. The next was very bright but not reliable. He had come to England for interview bringing an attractive young lady, 'his wife', but this was not the wife we found when we visited him in Germany. There was worse to come. He finally had an affair with the wife next door, in a Guildway house.

The distraught husband hanged himself on the banister rail and then our man moved in. He was concerned to assure us that he had had the sensitivity to replace the section of banister rail from which the late husband's demise took place.

The third time we got the right man. Entirely reliable, totally committed to Guildway, a real friend and a true gentleman: Walter Grisar from Antwerp, whose ancient family firm of commodity brokers was now in decline. Walter Grisar, educated at Dulwich, an elegant and friendly man who spoke perfect English, originally contacted Guildway to see whether he could help us to get established in Belgium: he had contacts who might be interested. He did not ask for any financial reward. From the start we all liked Walter and I well remember taking him round Loseley on the occasion of that first meeting.

Belgium was not an easy country for us and there was a problem with the two separate sectors, the French-speaking Walloons and the Dutch-speaking sector. Walter gave us a number of introductions in Belgium, including two Barons, one of whom was more interested in selling us equipment than in purchasing our houses; and the other, Baron Bracht, whose family entertained us most hospitably at their chateau, was tragically murdered. One of Walter's introductions did take on the distributorship and we sold a few houses in Belgium and even considered purchasing a large bankrupt joinery factory over there. Walter eventually took charge of our German company and got things into good order but very sadly died while still serving in Hamburg as our Geschäftsführer. We keep in touch with Karen, his widow, a sensitive person and a talented pianist who has sadly been semi-blind for many years.

We sold hundreds of houses in Germany but overall we did not make money and Germany had taken a great deal of our time which would have been more profitably used at home. Unfortunately there is no space to recount details of our experiences in which we learned a great deal about the Germans and their country. What impressed me above all was the fantastic way in which Germany recovered after the war. 'The German Miracle' is not an exaggeration. In 1946 Hamburg, like many German cities, was in ruins and a large population were living in bombed buildings and cellars and bordering on starvation. When we arrived in 1962, just sixteen years later, the city had been *completely* rebuilt and appeared prosperous.

There were follow-up visits to the USA and Denis Lockhart, then Works Superintendent, was authorised, on his American visit, to purchase a component cutter, only available from the American manufacturer. This complex machine, which we saw in several American factories, feeds timber through a gang of saws which are set at predetermined angles to give the needed cuts for the various components, giving a vast increase in productivity as well as improved accuracy; this was another 'first' for our company.

Our houses being no longer clad in cedar, the name 'Cedar Homes' was as misleading as had been 'Guildcrete' for cedar bungalows. We decided on a final name change to 'Guildway Limited', appropriate for any material. We always recognised the importance of communications and as early as 1961 started our quarterly publication *Guildway News*, which went out to builders, homeowners, building societies, architects, suppliers and friends. 1964 was one of our busier years, in which we launched our new two-storey local authority houses, erected at a government-sponsored exhibition, IBSAC, at the Crystal Palace. Industrialised housing had come a long way in the four years since our American tour and we now had several competitors. Some were large firms with substantial funding cutting margins to break into the market and often skimping on quality. At this time we started receiving enquiries from firms interested in purchasing our company. All were rejected, often over lunch, and we made some more friends.

Builders' Day that year was at the Civic Hall, Guildford, attended by over three hundred builders and we also held Regional Builders' Days at Brecon and Newmarket, where there were new developments with Guildway houses. Overseas we erected a house for British Week, Amsterdam.

The following year, 1965, saw the building of our new factory on the Artington site and the purchase of an eight-acre site for a proposed housing plant at Shildon, County Durham – a development area with grants and loans available. Shildon Council officials and members were most friendly and helpful. We built show houses and an information centre at Shildon, also used for meetings by the trade unions. We made many friends but sadly the housing market deteriorated and we had to sell the site.

In 1966 I appointed Fred Gooch as my Deputy Managing Director. Ever since Fred joined fourteen years earlier we had worked closely together. He was a great salesman, prepared to take endless trouble to give the customer what he wanted and he was also sound on technical matters. There were very few occasions when I failed to back Fred's judgment.

In 1971 Fred succeeded me as Managing Director with myself as Executive Chairman. The importance of openness, trust and mutual respect between the top people in a business cannot be overemphasised. I had a similar harmonious experience with Daphne Holloway in the less complex business of building up Loseley Dairy Products.

At Guildway we were developing in several directions at once – houses for developers, houses for individuals supplied through builders, local authority housing and special housing for the elderly as well as exports to many countries. Local authority housing contracts included 138 houses for Chailey, 73 for Blackburn, Lancs, 48 for Worthing, 130 for Pontypool, 25 for a Scottish Housing Association, 58 for Chichester, over 100 for Binscombe, Godalming. We shipped thousands of houses to local authorities. They were, of course, cheaper and plainer than our private sector housing but we did not compromise on standards of workmanship.

Home manufacturing is a complex business and the wider the variety of models and markets, the greater the complexity. The delivery schedules covered hundreds of separate items from nails, screws and washers to complete panels with the windows preglazed.

Aelfric Hudson visited fortnightly in his ancient Lanchester, its great virtue being its wide door which enabled the Canon, with considerable effort, to manoeuvre his large self with stiff leg out of the car. Aelfric was sensitive and did not go around quoting the Bible, just wandered round the factory having a word with anyone who turned to him and was available to hear any problems or grievances. Through the years we did try some Christian initiatives such as lunches with the Chaplain but they did not take on. Understandably, the non-church people did not come and many of the church people stayed away because they did not want to be labelled 'pious' or to be accused of currying favour with the Chairman.

Our one-time accountant and finance director sadly committed a serious breach of accountancy rules. When I took the appropriate action, he retorted: 'You call yourself a Christian, then you sack me.' He was a pleasant fellow and we all liked him but being a Christian is certainly not a permit to break the rules nor does it mean turning a blind eye to wrongdoing or being weak; quite the reverse. Although, for reasons of confidentiality, Aelfric was unable to pass on to me the content of most of his interviews, I know that he did help several people and some things which needed putting right were referred to me, with permission, and action was taken.

I learned a great deal about Christianity and business. In particular I discovered that I personally could best serve God in my business by being known as a Christian and, without reference to religion, striving to set an example and operate on Christian principles – having regard for truth, fairness, openness and showing consideration for individuals of all types and being compassionate to those in need. It was in compassion that I have felt led to serve and to minister in the name of Christ. When people are in trouble – sickness, bereavement, marriage breakdown, that is when they need help and that is the opportunity for giving them the most valuable help of all, awareness of God.

In 1971 we published *The Guildway Philosophy*, which may shock people who regard business purely as the making of money. It includes the following:

Our primary aim is not the making of money. Profit is essential for the growth and survival of the firm, the improvement of its service and the welfare of those who work in it.

We are ambitious. We want to develop at home and overseas as fast as conditions and resources will permit. We must be prepared to take calculated risks and we will always seek professional advice before embarking on any major project. We want to survive!

We appreciate the need for imagination, hard work, efficiency and the application of modern methods and techniques.

We aim to set an example in human relations within the firm and to maintain a close relationship with customers, suppliers and associates.

We work as a team and we want to remain 'a happy ship'.

CHAPTER 8

OVERSEAS AND OVER TO KELLY

One market where Guildway had no competition from other UK home manufacturers was exports. Following Germany, an early export order was for eight bungalows for Tortola in the British Virgin Islands. These were for holiday accommodation and Fred stayed there on one of his overseas sales journeys, and we also supplied some luxury houses to Tortola.

Distributors were established in France, Switzerland, Belgium, Holland, Luxembourg, Nigeria, the Channel Islands and Northern Ireland, with contacts in Iran and Algeria. Our French distributor, EGTP, headed by the tall and distinguished-looking Monsieur Rousseau, built a spectacular development, Le Village Anglais, at Pontault Combault near Paris. On its completion, we held our annual Distributors' Convention at Le Village, ending with a convivial evening in Paris at Le Lido.

There were often language problems. One difficult distributor arrived saying he was very 'ungry'. Plates of sandwiches were ordered but he declined to eat. It transpired that our friend was 'angry', not 'ungry'!

There were good distributors and not so good. Our first Swiss distributor failed to sell any houses and was always blaming our designs and prices, then Signor Bernasconi from Lugano took over and sales immediately grew to several houses a year. Our distributors were important members of the Guildway Club and we made many warm and enduring friendships, such as that with Walter Grisar, mentioned previously.

Fred and I, as well as our export staff, made visits to all the distributors; they visited us at Artington and we all met up at the annual Export Conventions.

Chief Adebayo Adetunji, always known as 'the Chief', was our Nigerian distributor. A large man, tall, extrovert, loud voice, usually a beaming smile – otherwise beware! Full of enthusiasm and energy, the Chief was a successful and influential man in Nigeria and had taken himself to Harvard Business School. When British Leyland built a factory in Nigeria the Chief got the contract to supply Guildway houses for the British directors and senior staff. Later he got us contracts for supplying a range of buildings to the International Institute for Tropical Agriculture at Ibadan and the Nigerian Customs and Excise at various locations, among other contracts.

The Chief was an enthusiastic supporter of our Distributors' Conventions. Fred spent several weeks in Nigeria and still has visits from the Chief, who has a Jaguar permanently based at Fred's Cedar Home at Compton. Fred and Doris were flown over as the Chief's guests to Nigeria for the wedding of his daughter. Fred has had some amazing experiences in faraway places in the service of Guildway.

We supplied 400 houses to Iran in the desert, rehousing families displaced from Tehran by one of the Shah's prestige re-developments. There were thousands of houses in this project and we were the only UK firm, the others being French, Canadian, Swedish and Japanese.

During a visit to Tehran I had a meeting with a Mr Gee, a National Bank chairman and adviser to the Shah, who offered to obtain contracts for us on 5 per cent commission. This led to our order for 250 houses. We were responsible for site work as well as delivery and erection of the packages. There were many problems and delays caused by legal complications regarding the land and underground watercourses. More serious was a letter demanding a sworn affidavit by me, stating that we had given no commissions, payments, bribes or inducements in respect of the contract. Mr Gee had already been paid his 5 per cent on the first shipment and I was certainly not going to commit perjury. I ignored the document. A stronger letter followed and on my next visit to Tehran I tackled Mr Gee in his office. He was contemptuous: 'This is just a small contract . . . does not apply . . .'

'It has got my name on it and my company's name and the details of our contract,' I replied. Mr Gee countered: 'We have done site work for you, we can include this as additional site work payment.' 'I am not prepared to accept that.' Thereupon Mr Gee told me to go and stop wasting his time. I consulted our Tehran lawyer who felt that he should get me an interview with the Prime Minister, Mr Horvat. Mr Gee would be disgraced and I felt that this should only be a last resort; I would continue to ignore the request to sign and hoped to complete the contract before further confrontation. To our great relief this proved to be the case. Prime Minister Horvat was hanged when the Ayatollah took over.

The packaged houses were delivered overland, a long and hazardous journey by lorry via Turkey. One of our lorries broke down, in the night the wheels were stolen, the load was looted and finally set on fire. We had suffered over the allocation of our sites, and then a more serious delay in the payment of our overdue accounts. We were short on finance and could not meet the erection costs without obtaining our stage payments. We gave notice of withdrawal from site and warned that we were suing for breach of contract. This produced a furious response and the demand for a meeting with me in Tehran. The meeting with the Managing Director, attended also by Robin, our Manager, was surprisingly harmonious. The MD stressed that if he paid us compensation, our competitors on the other sites, and his government, would be after him. Finally, after further discussion, the MD said: 'Let us reconvene tomorrow morning. I will work out the maximum that I can pay you and you work out the minimum that you are prepared to accept.'

As usual, I prayed about these matters and felt completely relaxed. Next morning, on our way to the meeting, Robin asked me what my figure was. 'I shall know when I sit down at the table,' I replied. The MD gave us a friendly welcome and asked my figure. '£240,000,' I replied. His figure was in Rials and he cranked the calculating machine. '£240,040,' he smilingly announced, adding: 'I'll give you the extra £40.' From then on there were no problems for us, the contract was completed just before the Shah was deposed and the Ayatollah Regime honoured the commitment to return the bonds.

After my return I mentioned to a visiting priest how good it was to be awakened at dawn by the call to prayer from the mosque. 'What a pity,' I added, 'that Christians do not have something similar.' 'But we do' asserted Father Brian: 'The Angelus, which we always ring in our Church at 6.00pm.'

A few weeks later a retired Anglican priest applied for a cottage. We had a cottage available and a vacancy for a minister to take the services at St Francis Littleton. Father John Clay had one request –

to toll the Angelus Bell in the church! John Clay, his wife Marjorie and daughter duly moved in and he tolled the Angelus Bell daily. Father John formed a Bible study group and a monthly group 'The Company of St Francis Littleton'. At our meetings, in one another's houses, we prayed and talked about people in hospital or needing help and discussed what we could do to help them and arranged visiting. People in hospital appreciated being visited by church members, some of whom they scarcely knew. A wife whose husband had left her was given firewood and other help. A husband whose wife was in hospital had lunches brought to him – on one occasion two ladies each bearing his lunch collided at his gate! These are typical examples of the Company of St Francis proving that the Church cared and offered help as well as prayer.

Guildway was awarded a contract in Algeria to replace 400 of the houses destroyed in the terrible earthquake at El Asnam. Fortunately there was no local commission involved, but like all overseas contracting jobs, there were problems – last-minute changes in specification, problems with sub-contractors, drums of paint were seen scurrying across the landscape: closer inspection revealed small boys underneath them! A local mosque is reputed to have been roofed with our galvanised sheeting.

In 1972 Guildway received the Queen's Award for Export Achievement. The presentation was made by the Lord Lieutenant with the whole company in attendance.

We entered into three overseas licensing agreements. The first was with Guildway (Ireland) Limited in 1967. Norman Reardon, the Chairman, was a delightful person with a sense of humour and, more important, a man to be trusted. In Ireland the pace is slower, standards are lower and there is less stress – unless you are in a hurry! Fred and I attended the opening of the factory in Middleton, County Cork, by Jack Lynch, Taoiseach (the Prime Minister). Norman recently informed us that Jack Lynch sadly suffered a stroke and is totally blind. To someone commiserating, he replied: 'But I'm so lucky to be able to hear.' Norman and Anne are devout Catholics and Norman assisted us in establishing a prayer network for the release of Dr Herrema, taken hostage by the IRA in Limerick in 1976. We got prayer going locally here and on an international level through my friend Mother General Mary Margaret SFDM and others. Norman became very active in this cause and I suspect that it was through him that

Dr Herrema, after his release, wrote to me with his personal thanks.

We also supplied houses to Northern Ireland, including Married Quarters at Hollywood Barracks, Lisburn, near Belfast. Fred and I and other members of the firm visited the Province a number of times, staying at the barricaded and several times bombed Europa Hotel, and our eyes were opened to the enormous inconvenience as well as the dangers suffered by the population of Belfast. Unlike war, which united a nation, there was nothing positive about the situation, no 'cause', just a feeling of helplessness, frustration and shame.

Back to the Middle East for the opening of the Saudi factory at Damman for production of Guildway houses by Kharafi, our licensees in Saudi Arabia. Tethered at the factory gate was a goat. As I suspected, this was not the company mascot, but lunch. A knife was wielded to its throat and the blood spilled forth in my honour. Thankfully I was spared the privilege of eating its eyes, though this would be preferable to the raw camel liver that Fred is reputed to have consumed in the Sudan 'for the honour of Guildway'. Kharafi, a large Kuwaiti civil engineering firm, also held the Guildway licence for Kuwait and I visited the factory there. As in Saudi Arabia, all office staff are male. There is a feudal atmosphere about Kuwait. The president of the company has his portrait in every office in the building and a large picture of him hangs at the end of the main corridor, under which sits the tea boy who brings round welcome cups of tea and cold drinks every half hour.

Ted Knaggs, from our technical department, worked for us in Arkansas and Iraq and spent several months in Kuwait and Saudi getting production under way and assisting with stock control procedures and technical advice. Dereck Sharpe from the works, Tony Zuk, technical manager, and Tim Dunford, technical sales, also carried out extended visits to assist setting up operations in the Middle East. Bruce Newman specialised in overseeing the construction of houses in hot desert places near the Saudi oilfields and in Bahrain and Nigeria. Joining us from school, Bruce became foreman in the Guildway factory. In Bahrain he turned down a number of invitations to leave his employment to work for other contractors at a greatly enhanced salary. In Europe it was Dave Nash who spearheaded the visits to the building sites and we were all delighted when Dave was awarded the BEM in recognition of this work. He still gets dozens of Christmas cards from homeowners as well as builders in France, Germany, Belgium and Holland.

Looking back, I am always amazed at how much we attempted and achieved. It seems we could never rest on our laurels, never say: 'Let's sit back and concentrate on improving what we are doing and on making some money.' There was always a challenge beckoning, new goals, new fields in which to lead. In our farm building days we claimed the widest range on the market and we could have made a similar claim for our housing with a wide choice of single-storey and two-storey housing: large luxury homes, housing for developers, local authority housing, special housing for the elderly, housing for export worldwide specially adapted to local requirements.

Among the thousands of families we housed, we included a countess, a number of bishops, a judge, an African chief, a Kuwaiti sheik – his was a magnificent luxury home, spacious rooms, marble-clad inside and outside, air conditioned; the adjoining staff quarters were built in unrendered concrete blocks, with tin roof, no insulation, no air conditioning. At home we supplied dozens of houses for the Crown Estates among many prestigious customers. One of our favourite customers was the Bishop of Guildford, George Reindorp, who purchased one of our houses for vacations and eventual retirement. The Bishop knew Canada well and was very keen on timber housing; he was always on the lookout for opportunities to publicise Guildway and signed his letters to us † 'George Guildway'.

What more could we do? We could expand beyond housing. As early as 1968 we had introduced doctors' surgeries and we supplied many of these in various parts of the country, as well as rectories which were less technically demanding. Many leading schools had sixth-form houses from Guildway, including Bradfield, Benendon, Down House, Heathfield, St Mary's Wantage, Wickham Abbey; and others, including Eton and Marlborough, had classrooms and laboratories and we supplied housing for the Universities of Surrey and Kent. We had particular satisfaction in supplying new buildings for Hydon Hill Cheshire Home – individual bedrooms for all the residents, bathrooms, kitchen, dining area and bar, shop and community centre. We also did a number of churches, community centres, village halls, church halls, clinics, motels and restaurants. And to think that it all started with flag poles and chicken coops!

I have mentioned our early financial problems and these were never far away. I make no apology for putting people before maximum profit but I now accept that I should have paid more attention to profit rather than expansion. The money supply I did take very seriously, spending time with the bank manager and, when required, with principal creditors.

About two years after the 'liquidation', a meeting was arranged at the head office of Westminster Bank in the City. John Owers, our financial adviser, and Meryn Lewis accompanied me to the meeting with Mr Adams, the General Manager of the Bank. We needed an additional £10,000 overdraft for Guildcrete. 'I'm sorry, I cannot increase your limit for Guildcrete. I could allow Loseley an additional £10,000. It's up to you, but in my view you would be most unwise to transfer it.' The wisdom of Solomon! I have always been grateful to Mr Adams.

Not long afterwards Guildway needed a further £10,000. This time I went to see my friend Paul Getty at Sutton Place. I explained the position as we paced the Long Gallery with its lovely pictures, and then sat on the window seat at the end. Eventually, Paul agreed to make the loan, for a six-month period, subject to my delivering to Sutton Place the most valuable contents of the Loseley Drawing Room for the duration of the loan. Unless the loan was repaid within six months the objects would pass to Getty. We managed to repay the loan just before the six months period came up and we welcomed back the Drawing Room furniture with great relief.

Loseley and Guildway were closely linked: the company rented and then purchased the site from Loseley. The double-glazing of all the ground floor Loseley House windows was done by Guildway, recorded by a plaque on the Drawing Room windows. John Sillence, one of our earliest Guildway members, carried out the work. He started in the concrete mould shop as his first job after national service and remained with us for the rest of his working life. He was a great character.

The plaque in the Long Gallery states: 'This Gallery was restored by removal of partitions erected 1820 for staff bedrooms by Guildway Limited, Michael Knight, Alec Berry and Dick Schofield for James and Sue More-Molyneux in 1974.'

One cannot speak of work on Loseley House without mentioning the name of Peter Bridger. Peter is a remarkable craftsman in virtually all building materials. On many occasions his solutions have impressed the architects and structural engineers. Peter led the major restoration programme from 1981 to 1985 covering stone work, structural timbers, roofing and valleys, gutters, joists and beams, floors, panelling, plaster work, plumbing etc. On completion Peter Bridger made and presented to us a splendid wooden casket in the form of a book containing a detailed account of the work and names of the nineteen men involved. Peter Bridger had joined Guildway in 1954 and in March 1990 transferred to Loseley and he has been working on Loseley House ever since.

Several barns, poultry houses and other buildings on the Estate were supplied by Guildway and some cottage conversions were carried out by them, all at cost. I received no salary in the years when we made no profit and a very modest one when we were profitable, and the company never paid a dividend. They did supply my cars, all secondhand and cherished. They lasted on average for ten years, and Sue and I were always sad to part with them, especially Lil the BMW 3.0 csi after twenty years and 200,000 miles.

I liked to spend a day with each of the fourteen Area Managers as well as visiting overseas distributors. On two occasions these Guildway visits produced new members for the Loseley team. With Ken Watters, the Scottish Area Manager, one appointment was in Glasgow with a developer building Guildway houses on the Isle of Bute. When we arrived at the appointed hour the office was deserted. We waited with increasing impatience until a nice blonde lady arrived, full of apologies: her husband had suffered a heart attack. She, Nancy Smith, would take us over to the Island, give us lunch and show us the houses under construction. It was a lovely sunny day, Nancy's hospitality was splendid and the Island provided a delightful setting for our houses. Despite her husband's very serious condition – sadly he died shortly afterwards – Nancy insisted on escorting us back to the ferry, bestowing on us packages of local smoked kippers.

A year or two after this, Nancy's younger daughter Linda came and stayed with us for a period of work experience at Guildway. Sometime afterwards Nancy herself called on us with son Johnny on the way to a visit in Salisbury. Sue mentioned that we had a vacancy for someone to do some cooking and to provide teas for the public, and if Nancy ever heard of anyone suitable we would be grateful if she would let us know. Some months later Nancy wrote offering her services. Sue wrote at once accepting the offer, Nancy was soon installed in one of our cottages and provided wonderful meals for us, teas for the public, and became a real friend.

Another valuable team member for Loseley was recruited by me on a visit to Area Managers in the West Country. As dusk was falling one summer evening, I was driving along a country lane in Dorset, near Sixpenny Handley village, and asked a lone pedestrian if he could advise me where to stay the night. He warmly recommended the King John in the village. It was small but bright and clean, like Joan Newman, who greeted me warmly. Her husband Cyril was serving cheerfully in the bar and there was a good atmosphere; dinner was excellent and before retiring I was given a form to fill in my breakfast requirements. Breakfast was excellent and precisely as ordered. Before leaving I said to Joan Newman: 'If you ever give up this place do let us know. I'm sure we could find something for you.' Sue and I went down to the King John for a weekend and Sue shared my enthusiasm. About a year later Joan wrote that they had decided to give up the pub. They duly moved to Stable Cottage, Loseley, and took on the teas for the public, baking the cakes and running the shop.

Sometimes I wonder if Loseley would have been better off if I had stuck to my idea at the age of 17 and developed the canning and processing of Loseley organic vegetables. With the same dedicated effort that Fred and I and the team put into Guildway, anything would have been possible. Although, with Sue, I have always been dedicated to the survival of Loseley, I have not shown the same dedication to the making of money. It was through the financial problems of Guildway that I became fully aware of the reality of God, and it was at Guildway that I first testified to my Christian faith, leading to my deep personal experience of God. Because through Guildway I had been brought closer to God, I felt that the company must survive at all costs. I now realise that I was wrong in thinking this.

In 1973 we had an exceptionally good year with 1,175 houses sold and a profit of over £300,000. That year we held talks with County Bank, the NatWest Merchant Bank, regarding the flotation of Guildway as a public company within the next two years. Going public: a fantastic thought! For years we had been thankful to escape liquidation. Going public was beyond our dreams; at last Loseley would be adequately funded. We were advised by the top people at the Bank and entertained to delightful lunches. Everyone was most kind and helpful.

Success is sweet but ours was short-lived. Next year, the world oil crisis hit us. The boom was over and Guildway plunged into loss. No more help from County Bank. No more lunches. Competition was increasing, margins being squeezed to get orders. I began to realise that we must sell the company to ensure its survival. My first choice was Redland, suppliers of the roof tiles for our houses, with whom we had a long and sound relationship. The Chairman, Sir Colin Corness, came round our factory and offices and lunched at Loseley with Sue and me. He said that he was impressed with what he had seen of Guildway but the decision would have to be made by his Take-Overs Committee and they might not consider that we were quite large enough. Sadly, this proved to be the case.

In this period there were some changes. Fred's lovely wife Joan died of cancer in 1976 and the following year, at his request, Fred handed over as MD to Dr John Bailey and took on again the position of Export Director, spending several active months in Nigeria and the Middle East. This was significant because at that time half our business was overseas. Geoffrey Gilbertson, soon to be knighted for his work for the disabled, a friend from army days, and retired ICI Head of Personnel, joined the Board as Non-Executive Director. Geoffrey was a giant of a man, with determination to match his 6ft 6ins height. He had suffered from polio in the late 1940s and since then had been in a wheelchair. Michael Fenton-Jones, past Chairman of Commercial Union Properties and other companies and a well-known Christian evangelist, also joined the Board as a Non-Executive Director.

By now we were really under pressure. Sales were declining and I did not have the same rapport with the new MD as I had enjoyed for so long with Fred. Geoffrey lived in County Durham and had introduced Dr Bailey, the new MD. Michael lived locally and was uneasy about the new management. It was not a happy period: we had lost the momentum and the unity. Too many people telling me what I should do. I did know that Michael had special powers of Christian discernment and I did not always listen to him as I should have done; he resigned in spring 1982.

Fred Gooch retired on his 65th birthday in June 1982 and I appointed him Life President of Guildway. On the same day I terminated Dr Bailey's contract and took over again the running of the company myself. For the next few months I enjoyed being in control once more but I realised that a full-time MD was needed.

One day Simon Oppenheimer came to see me on another matter. Simon was MD of a larger company in the area, manufacturing a product which had become superseded by plastics and Simon had the unenviable job of closing down his company. Sue and I had met Simon and his wife Mairi on a number of occasions previously: we got on well and I respected Simon's forthright integrity. He was a tidy, well-organised person and I knew I would be able to rely on him. I tentatively mentioned the vacant position to Simon; his response was cautious but about three months later he took over as Managing Director and I continued as Executive Chairman.

It was encouraging that in 1982 we returned to profitability and I felt happier about the future. Then, from a completely unexpected quarter, disaster struck: it struck not just Guildway but the whole timber-frame housing industry. We had met with the 'unacceptable face of capitalism' working through the media. The Brick and Block Manufacturers' Association had become concerned at losing business through the advance of brick skin timber-frame housing, the system Fred and I had brought from the USA. Wimpey, Barratt and many other developers had switched from concrete blocks to timber frame. We supplied all Wimpey and Barratt houses in our region.

The Brick and Block people briefed a PR firm to taint the image of timber-frame housing. They hit the jackpot with ITV's *World In Action.* The programme urged home buyers to make sure that the home they were buying was 'a traditional masonry house, not a wood frame house with bricks on the outside'. 'We all know that wood rots,' the voice warned. 'Wood catches fire.' Then: 'Sir Laurie Barratt's dry construction' accompanied by shots of panels lying in mud, the rain pouring down. Completely one-sided, not one good point, no interviews with home occupiers, who would certainly have enthused. As a result of that programme orders for timber-frame houses were cancelled all over the country. 'It isn't timber frame, is it?' The reply that timber-frame houses are so warm, engineered, no cracks, 90 per cent of all houses in the USA are timber frame, fell on deaf ears.

In 1960 Guildway had built the first manufactured brick skin timber-frame house in the UK. By 1984 timber-frame brick skin accounted for 24 per cent of all housing starts. No wonder the block makers were worried. Within two months of *World In Action*, the figure had fallen from 24 per cent to 5 per cent and it took at least ten years before the market fully recovered. Builders and developers could not sell their timber-frame houses, several went into liquidation and so did home manufacturers. Guildway lost £500,000 that year and the overdraft shot up to £1,600,000.

With the industry reeling from the blow, there was little hope of finding a buyer for a timber-frame house manufacturer. With a splendid twelve-acre site on a main road, I could have put Guildway Limited into voluntary liquidation and sold the site for at least £6,000,000. I just would not do that, though it would have been sensible. I had repeatedly stated: 'people are more important than money'. Tim Perkins, Chairman of Sandell Perkins, builders' merchants, had made a good offer for Guildway, but, as a friend, he pointed out that the site value was much greater than the worth of the company as a going concern. Any purchaser would re-sell the site and Tim did not want to be the one to do it: he understood my feelings.

There was one person who still believed in timber-frame construction. A large, bearded Irishman, Declan Kelly, had been a Guildway customer as a developer for two years, taking houses for developments in London and the Home Counties. Kelly was interested in buying Guildway and moving the staff of his development company into our offices. We also had a local entrepreneur showing interest and although his financial standing was dodgy I felt he might be useful. Kelly could be genial but was a tough man to deal with. One day we had a very difficult session with Declan going back on his previous undertaking, trying to browbeat me into reducing the price. Soon after returning home that evening, the Loseley burglar alarm went off; I could not silence it and eventually I had to wrench it off its mountings and smother it in blankets. Into my head came the message: 'Kelly is trying to steal Guildway.'

Next morning I rang Declan and said: 'The deal is off.' He at once started talking of misunderstandings, that he was prepared to improve his offer. 'No, I'm selling to someone else.' Next day Kelly's MD rang Glye Hodson, my friend and consultant, and told him that he and Declan were very concerned about me and felt that I must be mentally unstable to turn down their offer. He invited Glye to dinner two days later in London. Sue and I also happened to be in London that evening, receiving a Countryside Commission Award. I telephoned Kelly's office and made an appointment to see him at 7pm.

When I arrived Kelly eagerly enquired: 'Does this mean . . .?' 'It means I'm taking you out to dinner,' I replied. Glye Hodson, already in the office, was surprised to see me. He also happily accepted my invitation and so did the MD who had expected to be hosting Glye. Kelly drove me to the restaurant in his Rolls and the two others joined us there. It was a relaxed and enjoyable meal at the Marquis Restaurant. After a couple of hours we had agreed on the deal; I had gained a few concessions as well as a considerable increase in the price. The Loseley burglar alarm had done its stuff. A pity Declan had not got a burglar alarm on the Rolls, for when he unlocked the boot to retrieve our coats and briefcases, they had gone and the lock was undamaged. The deal was signed on 2nd January 1985.

Declan Kelly kept Guildway going for four years and then sold the company to the directors on their undertaking to vacate the site within three months. Guildway moved to a factory at Bordon. Sadly, after two years the firm went into receivership but was then purchased by Meyer International Timber Plc, who had been one of our major suppliers. Soon afterwards, having sold the site for some £8 million, the Declan Kelly Group went bankrupt owing £200 million. In a typical comment, ex-Guildway Director Stephen Davies commented: 'We did sometimes make losses, but nothing like that. We just didn't think big enough!'

The show still goes on, though the chaps always tell me it is not the same. We pensioners meet at funerals and at the annual summer get-together at Loseley. We have some wonderful memories, moments of triumph and disaster.

We had a splendid record of long service with well over half the labour force having more than ten years' service and several over twenty-five years. Guildway had three company gatherings every year – the Summer Garden Party at Loseley to which all members of Loseley and Guildway and pensioners were invited; the Social Club Winter Dance, which was always an enjoyable occasion, and I never saw anyone seriously the worse for drink.

Every Christmas Eve we had a gathering of all members of the firm in the canteen – around a hundred people present, together with Sue and the Honorary Chaplain. I always gave a talk about the main issues, the events of the past year and our future plans. On the last and nostalgic occasion I am told that my unscripted talk lasted forty minutes. I mentioned that my Christian faith had developed more as a result of Guildway trauma than anything which happened in church: I hastened to add that I was not suggesting that they should not go to church, quite the opposite, but that it is in the ups and downs of life that we can become aware of the reality of God. Later that day, calling on the Bishop of Guildford, Michael Adie, to present a Christmas ice-cream gateau, I told him what I had told the company about the growth of my faith through Guildway. Sadly this was not well received by my Bishop, although it did not prevent him, soon afterwards, from approving my appointment as a lay pastoral assistant and as a server at the Eucharist.

In January 1985 I ended my farewell message in *Guildway News* with:

> Greatest of all the blessings I have received through Guildway is the increase in my Christian faith and spiritual awareness. The light does shine in the darkness; the impossible can happen if we have the humility to be open to God. I have been privileged to experience this in a number of critical situations through the years. Through Guildway I also had my first experience of the power of prayer in healing. Man is body, mind and spirit and if we fail to acknowledge our spiritual nature we shall never be fully alive and we deprive ourselves of God's love and His inner peace at times of stress, strife, sorrow and death. Neither the affluent society nor the technological revolution can replace God. Fred and I foresaw the housing revolution; with even greater anticipation I await the spiritual revolution.

The wording below is on the plaque on the magnificent 20ft totem pole at Orange Court Farm, Loseley. Fred Gooch set up the Canadian log in his garden and for over six years worked on carving and painting, having researched all the correct Red Indian designs and paints.

THE LOSELEY TOTEM POLE

This Cedar log grew on Vancouver Island, B.C.
It was presented by Messrs. MacMillan Bloedel and Montague Meyer
and carved and painted by Mr. Fred Gooch for Loseley

to commemorate 30 years of pioneering
timber frame manufactured housing in the U.K.,
using Canadian timber,
by James More-Molyneux and Fred Gooch,
with the firm which they founded – Guildway Limited.

A valued relic of the West and of the past,
the totem pole, unlike the Christian symbol below,
has no religious significance.

Unveiled on June 8th 1988

by

Mr. GARDE B. GARDOM, Q.C.
Agent General for B.C.

The Christian symbol also forms an introduction to the next
chapter.

CHAPTER 9

FAITH

'You are lucky, you have faith. I go to church because it is good for the children and I enjoy the singing . . .' That was in 1957 and my friend, a brewery director, and I were returning from a Christian Business Discussion Group. It had not occurred to me that people who did not believe would be churchgoers, but my friend did want to find faith. Years later we met again and I was thrilled to find that he had become a man of deep faith – and by then so had I. We are all on a spiritual journey and conversion can be immediate, dramatic or gradual. It is on offer to everyone.

A significant incident on my Christian journey occurred less than five months after I 'nailed my colours to the mast', giving my testimony at Guildway in 1958. It resulted from it, as if it were God's response to my initiative at the opening of our offices by Canon Hudson.

It is not easy to talk of direct personal experience of God. Joseph, in the Old Testament, discovered this when he told his brothers about his dreams and they planned to kill him. In my case it was not fear but awe and humility that made it difficult for me to speak of my experience of God, even to my family, for years after it happened. As time passed I have felt led to share it, aware that the experience was given not just for me, but to help others to find a deeper faith. Faith, it is said, can be caught, not taught. It can only be caught, though, by those open and willing to receive it.

For ten days in June 1958 Sue, Mike our seven-year-old son, and I were staying as paying guests at 'Tandalar', our friend Vicky Cooke's Welsh cottage in the lovely Mawddach Estuary near Dolgellau. This was an ideal spot for our holidays when Mike was young, and we came here annually for about ten years. We climbed Cader Idris, the mountain we could see from our windows, and walked on lesser hills. We found a beach between

Barmouth and Harlech with lovely sand dunes; we had the place to ourselves but sometimes black cattle would saunter onto the beach to claim their rights of occupancy.

24th June 1958 was a lovely sunny day and we had been swimming in the sea and basking in the sand dunes. Lazing on the sand with Sue and Mike that morning, I was reading an account of the Lambeth Conference, currently taking place. Anglican bishops from all over the world were assembled to discuss important issues affecting the Church. I put the paper down and my thoughts continued about God and the world.

I had a strong and unquestioning faith in Almighty God – Father, son and Holy Spirit. I worshipped Him, I prayed to Him, I believed. But lying there in the sun, the thought suddenly came: 'How wonderful it would be if one could be absolutely certain.' On an impulse, I silently asked God to change to red the colour of a piece of sand which I touched. A childish thing to do and I did not really expect the sand to change colour. It didn't and I put it out of my mind and continued reading. After a picnic tea, we returned to Tandalar for a bath and change. After supper I usually went out on my own for a walk and to pray. Praying outside at night was a habit I had picked up in the war – the vast stillness of the desert, the clear star-spangled sky, the moonlight: a sense of awe, an awareness of the vastness of Creation, a depth of stillness. A wonderful setting for prayer.

On that June evening in 1958, the Welsh valley was particularly lovely: a clear sky, soft fading sunlight. I walked along the riverbank, then across the road to a footpath leading up the hill. As I approached the hill I was suddenly aware of a strange and wonderful sensation. Love was pouring into my head. I had never experienced anything like this before, nor have I since. It continued for several seconds, this in-pouring of love. Where did it come from and why? I walked on up the hill, a young plantation of fir trees on the left and a low dry-stone wall to the right, with a view in the now fading light across the river valley to the hills beyond. I halted and began to pray.

Immediately I became aware of the presence of God. He was close to me on my left side. I did not look round, for I knew that I should not see Him with as great certainty as I knew that He was present. Over the years I have heard the question: 'What would you do if Jesus entered the room now?' I now know the answer. On that Welsh hillside, aware of God's presence, I immediately fell to my knees. No words, I was just filled with awe and reverence. Then suddenly I was flooded with light; glorious bright gold and silver light flooded through my head and immersed my being. I was aware that I was experiencing the glory of God. I do not know how long I stayed on my knees but eventually I got up and continued the walk up the hill. I was now aware that the love that had poured in was God's love, followed by His presence and then His glory: a three-part experience. He had, I felt certain, made Himself known to me for a purpose.

As I walked I gave thanks to God and prayed that He would make known what He wanted me to do, expecting an instant response. I walked slowly on . . . halted for a minute or two . . . walked on again alert, full of expectancy . . . halted . . . It was getting dark now, Sue would be worried and I made my way back to the cottage. By next morning I still had no answer.

God's timing is different from ours and I had to wait a further eighteen years. In the meantime I was aware that there was plenty of room for improvement in my life: while waiting for God to make known His purpose, I had to try harder to live in accordance with His will. It also came into my mind that I should attend services at churches of different denominations – Roman Catholic, Anglo-Catholic, Methodist, Baptist, Non-Conformist and, for good measure, I attended services at a Christian Science church and a synagogue, as well as joining with Sue in regular worship at our own C. of E. churches at St Nicholas Compton and St Francis Littleton. I spent time with monks and nuns, discussed religion with clergy, especially Guildway's Honorary Chaplain, Aelfric Hudson; I went on retreats, spent more time in prayer, attended talks and I read Christian books, not many because I was so busy with both Guildway and Loseley.

It was my duty to restore Loseley and to build it up and Guildway was now equally important, having survived – thanks to God's grace. It seemed that for several years ahead business must be my priority and expanding businesses are time-demanding. Meanwhile I was attempting to serve God through Loseley and Guildway. We shared our profits with all employees, we aimed to set high standards of integrity and straight-dealing, and Guildway had their Hon. Chaplain. At Loseley there was the additional awareness of our responsibility as stewards of God's Creation, with concern for the wellbeing of our livestock and the health of the soil.

Why was I suddenly so keen about God and evangelism? I was not brought up to this: in pre-war days it was not the done thing. Religion was church on Sundays, keep the Commandments, be kind and helpful, set an example. The rector was responsible for the wellbeing of the parish and he could be left to get on with it. My father had been Churchwarden for many years and my mother was a devout Christian, but talk about religion was not encouraged and my parents would have been uneasy about my evangelism. These were the attitudes of the pre-1939 era. I am not criticising my parents: I am thankful to them for my Christian upbringing.

So why was I so keen? I think the answer is that having now experienced the reality of God, at a deeper level, I felt the deep need to share my love of God with others. That experience was real and can never be taken from me. I have no doubt whatever: I know that it was Almighty God, Father, Son and Holy Spirit. I was on my way to pray to Him when His love poured in. It was His presence that I felt, His glory that I experienced. God is real. My longing to bring others to share my awareness of God did not stem from one-upmanship: quite the reverse, for it was years before I felt able to tell anyone about that experience in Wales, though it had a deep effect on my life from the moment it occurred.

Evangelising at Loseley was even more difficult than at Guildway. At first I did not realise that the real problem was me! I suggested to Colin, then the tractor driver foreman, that we might have a Rogation Day Service in the farmyard, with the blessing by the Rector of the fields and animals. Colin gave a very firm but polite: 'Please not.' With hindsight I can now understand and Colin was right. If these things are laid on by the boss, tension is caused. Those who attend will be open to accusations of currying favour with the employer. I bowed to Colin's judgment and reluctantly dropped the matter.

I believed that Guildway had been saved from liquidation through the strength and guidance which God provided – the human experts had pronounced liquidation as inevitable. I had dedicated Guildway to God, which made me even more determined that it should survive and build a reputation. This had a significant effect on future decisions and through Guildway I was to experience God at a deeper level on three significant occasions, including my early healing ministry.

Eventually it was at Loseley that we were able to evangelise openly and minister in the name of the Lord. Not to the staff, but to the visiting public, to Christian groups and above all with the Loseley Christian Cancer Help Centre. Loseley was to become not only home to eight members of the family in three generations, an historic house open to the public, the trademark on the Dairy Products, but also a recognised Christian Centre.

In 1960 the Loseley Christian Centre was two decades away. At this stage, following my experience of God, I was searching for His purpose and getting frustrated at the lack of success of my efforts at evangelism. I learned to be patient, to trust God and I learned more about prayer. Like most people, I had not been taught about prayer since the days of 'God bless Mummy and Daddy.' Prayer is a vital part of our relationship with God. If we love someone we need to converse with them, listening as well as speaking and, best of all, just being silently aware of their presence. That is what I have come to know as prayer.

There is so much misunderstanding about Christianity: it is not just about church services, boring sermons, it is not just negative: 'Thou shalt not.' God is loving and compassionate. He longs for us to accept Him and I believe that anyone who is open and truly desires to find faith in God can do so.

We are all at different stages on the spiritual journey, there are different levels of faith and of commitment but each one of us has scope for deepening our faith, coming closer to God. It is a long road; at times it is hard but all who undertake the journey are sustained by prayer and by fellow-travellers. I have mentioned spending time with monks and nuns, for these are people of faith and deep commitment to God. They are also people of humility and, just as 'humus' in the soil is necessary for healthy plant growth, so is 'humility' essential for healthy spiritual growth.

There is a wide diversity of Religious Orders, still including a few Closed Orders, whose members shut themselves off from the world, devoting themselves to prayer and the presence of God. Members of Closed Orders do vital work, including acting as spiritual directors to other monks and nuns, bishops, clergy and others. Members of other Orders go out visiting, teaching, preaching, leading retreats, running hospitals, nursing and looking after the homeless, single parents and others in need. There are no barriers of race and I know of a home for the terminally ill in Asia, run by the Roman Catholic Order of St Francis and the Divine Motherhood, where nearly all the patients are Moslems. The Mother House – the HQ – of this Order, SFDM, is at Godalming with hospitals and houses staffed by nuns at a number of places in the UK and Ireland, as well as in Africa, America, Asia and Australia.

I had the privilege of helping in the management of the SFDM's farm near Godalming. Nuns are excellent at gardening and tending poultry, sheep, pigs and rearing calves but a large dairy herd is more complex, with herdsman, silage contractors, feed merchants, inseminators . . . and eventually I advised Mother General to give up farming and we let the land to a local farmer.

Sue and I were privileged to have a close friend in Mary Margaret, Mother General of the Order. She was quite a jet-setter, flying off to her outposts around the world; Irish, full of fun and with a real sparkle, mirroring her great love, particularly love of the Lord. Despite strict discipline and being under the vow of Chastity, Poverty and Obedience, love and joy are at the heart of the Franciscan Orders.

Mary Margaret was a great encouragement to me in my growing faith and occasionally I had the privilege of participating in evening prayer in the Convent Chapel, as the only male, the only Anglican, the only lay person in the congregation. In her last years, Sister Margaret as she now was, had become very frail with poor eyesight, but she never complained. Her favourite response to any good news was: 'Praise God!' On the last visit I made, Margaret was very infirm and could hardly walk but insisted on accompanying me from her room to the front door to see me off. She was so frail, I could not leave her there to get back unaided, so I accompanied her back to her room, then she returned to the door with me . . . I am not sure how many times this went on but I made certain that finally I left her safely in her room. It was largely through the influence of Mother Mary Margaret that I myself became a Novice in the Third Order of St Francis (SSF).

I have always revered St Francis. He loved all of Creation because above all he loved God, the Creator. In addition to his Friars, he founded a lay branch of the Order, known as the Third Order. There are rules, including prayer, worship, work and study. It was here that I learned the importance of a minimum time of daily prayer, my minimum being half an hour, usually considerably more. There are talks, meetings and special services. Ordained ministers act as chaplains and spiritual directors and, with others, as novice counsellors. In the Third Order rules are tailored appropriately to individual members according to circumstances. Simplicity is significant to the Franciscan along with the very important objective 'To make our Lord known and loved'. One of the benefits of membership is the fellowship with other committed Christians. An example of the flexibility of the rules is that of an elderly widow in a wheelchair, who said to me: 'I am not able to work or visit the sick like you but I do spend a long time in prayer. Just let me know your prayer requests.' In a chapter on 'Faith' one should also mention works, for it is 'by their deeds that ye shall know them'. Christians are judged more on what they do and how they behave than on what they say.

Sue and I had been on retreats under Father Toby Manson SSJE (Society of St John the Evangelist). We got to know Father Manson quite well and in his later years he spent his summer vacations with us at Loseley. He had served under my father in the First World War and was awarded the MC for gallantry. Toby Manson was short, lean, with twinkling eyes, full of fun and a vast fund of 'shaggy dog' stories. 'What do you get if you put boiling water down a rabbit hole?' . . . 'Hot cross bun!' Once when Toby Manson visited us we had a litter of Labrador puppies. We named the black pup that we were keeping 'Toby' after Father Toby Manson, who always wore the black gown and beret of SSJE. Telephoning soon afterwards, he announced himself: 'It's the black puppy from Oxford!' Beneath the surface humour was deep spirituality, profound wisdom and understanding and through him many people besides ourselves were helped in their spiritual development. He gave the address at my father's Memorial Service. When officiating at a Communion Service he was steeped in holiness – his bearing, the slow, precise movements, the prayers audible yet almost whispered, so great was the depth of his awe and reverence.

Father James Naters SSJE is now the Superior of the Order. James played an important part in the development of the Loseley Christian Centre and he is also a link with the past. I have mentioned in an earlier chapter my discussion at the age of 10 in the Yellow Dormitory with Charles Wylie. Some fifty years on, Sue and I were privileged to be present when James Naters officiated at the wedding of Charles Wylie and Sheila Green, a St Thomas' nursing sister who had looked after Charles's first wife, Diana, who sadly died of cancer. Sheila, with Charles, now runs a Julian Prayer Group. Charles, after serving as a Ghurka Officer in the war and a spell as a Japanese Prisoner of War, went on to be British Pentathlon Champion and a member of Lord Hunt's successful Everest Expedition and initiated the Ghurka Appeal, and is still involved in welfare work including Nepal and the Ghurkas. He was appointed OBE in 1995.

Many people, including myself, find retreats helpful in developing their faith. Retreats are usually held from Friday evening until the Sunday afternoon in a convent, monastery or a special retreat house. Normally silence is kept and often recorded music is played during meals; sometimes there is a reading, recorded talk or sermon. The retreat conductor is usually a monk or an ordained minister. There are a number of addresses and short services, often finishing with the night office of Compline which ends the day with great peace, placing ourselves and our homes under God's protection. Retreats are becoming increasingly popular and some are now specially tailored for people who have not yet found faith in God. Returning home to the world after a silent retreat is less dramatic than re-entering earth's atmosphere from outer space, but it is quite a shock!

I had a special encounter with a nun on a visit to the Vatican for Guildway. I was visiting a Monseigneur, one of Reverend Mother Mary Margaret's contacts, about housing for Christian villages in the Lebanon. His opening words were: 'You know what today is?' '22nd June,' I replied. 'It's Thomas More's Day!' I felt that this happy coincidence merited my receiving Communion in the great Vatican Church of St Peter's: St Thomas More would surely approve. It was a deeply moving experience.

After the service I was standing in the main aisle of St Peter's, looking down the vast building to the sanctuary. A shaft of light from the dome window emphasised the sanctity. A group of nuns, solemn, devout, were walking slowly up the centre aisle. One appeared to be praying her rosary. As they got nearer I caught the eye of the little nun on the side nearest me, very young and not very tall, with bright eyes and dark-coloured skin. On impulse I felt the need to share the depth of spirituality which I sensed at that moment: I smiled, but instead of the hoped-for response, came an expression of embarrassment, resentment. A split-second later the answering smile came. I knew that she understood: we had shared that sacred moment.

Year after year, mixed with the challenges of Loseley and Guildway, my Christian preparation phase continued: retreats, talks, books and, most important of all, prayer.

We are not all called to serve God in the same way. As St Paul tells us in 1 Corinthians 12, there are many gifts of the Spirit – to one wisdom is given, to another discernment, to others faith, gifts of healing, miracle working, speaking in tongues, interpreting tongues. These gifts are still given today, for the benefit of the Church, the members working together just as in the time of the apostles. It is unfortunate that some charismatics who have been given gifts such as 'speaking in tongues' consider as spiritually inferior people who have not received that gift. Such people lack the humility essential to a true Christian and they cause hurt to individuals and to the cause of Christ. I did not consider myself in any way superior and for years I did not even speak of my spiritual experience, though obviously Sue was aware that I was suddenly spending more time with God. Before that day in Wales in June 1958, Sue and I had been as one in our worship, and now I was going to meetings and on retreats which at the time Sue did not feel were for her.

A less dedicated wife would have put me under pressure or labelled me a religious fanatic. It is not often that husband and wife share their initial deep spiritual experiences at the same time. Sue was always supportive and she was to find her own role before long and we have both been richly blessed.

One of the times when I felt led to share my 1958 experience of God was some thirty years after that evening in Wales and it started at a funeral. John Dixey was a close and loyal friend before and during the war. John had told me about his friend John Dee, completely paralysed by a stroke. His wife, Elizabeth, had dedicated her life to nursing her husband at home, also working part-time. John, Elizabeth's husband, was completely incapacitated and could not speak, move his hands or legs or do any function for himself. Elizabeth had to wash, dress and feed him, get him up, in and out of bed, everything. John Dixey died not long after telling me this moving story and I attended his funeral in Suffolk. Processing from the church through the village to the burial ground, I found myself next to a youngish lady: slim, not very tall and rather shy, who turned out to be Elizabeth Dee.

I arranged to visit Elizabeth and her husband in their little flat in a Sussex town. John showed no sign of recognition and was unaware that I was speaking to him, yet I felt at ease and found myself talking to Elizabeth about the Lord. Elizabeth responded that she had been brought up a Roman Catholic but had opted out when she was 17 and that was that. I told her of my faith in God and of my Welsh experience, adding that I felt certain that this had been given to be shared with others. Before leaving I gave Elizabeth a copy of Bishop Morris Maddocks's *A Healing House of Prayer*.

A short time after my visit Elizabeth wrote saying that her mother had died but in her last minutes Elizabeth had been able to tell her: 'I'm going to church again.' A faint smile came to her mother's lips: 'I'm so pleased,' she whispered and she died in great peace. Elizabeth's husband, John, died peacefully in hospital in 1991. We have faith that our prayers have been answered, that John is at peace and in God's glory.

Elizabeth daily attends Mass at her church, where she became a founder member of a healing prayer group and is now on the parochial church council and deanery synod. She has a disciplined prayer life and is involved in compassionate work apart from her full-time social service employment, assisting disabled people. Consecrating her life to God, Elizabeth has progressed further in faith and works in four years than I have in forty.

Throughout the world, countless monks and nuns in the Religious Orders are giving their lives to the service of God. Also helping us to deepen our faith is the example of the Christian Saints and Martyrs. Rather than renounce Jesus Christ, thousands through the ages have accepted torture and terrible deaths: being thrown to the lions, roasted alive, crucified. Over the past few years with the fall of communism in Eastern Europe we are seeing a great outpouring of hunger for the Word of God. Visitors to Poland, Russia and other liberated countries are thrilled to witness the packed churches, the joy and enthusiasm of the worshippers. How we need that enthusiasm, that joy! Greater still is the need for a purpose to life and not insignificant is the promise of life after death. God still offers us these gifts, yet so many reject Him.

A very wealthy man once said to me: 'Being a good neighbour, helping people: that's what Christianity is, isn't it?' My answer, of course, was: 'No.' Being a good neighbour is the essence of the second commandment: 'Love they neighbour as thyself', amplified by our Lord in the story of 'The Good Samaritan'. But the first and great commandment is: 'Thou shalt love the Lord thy God with all thy mind, with all thy heart, with all thy soul and with all thy strength.' For years I had difficulty with this: I did love God but how could I love Him above everything else at His command? It did not seem reasonable. Then, after I had felt His love pouring into me, it was natural to respond by loving Him. If we can feel God's great love for us, remembering the sacrifice He made for us on the cross, it is not difficult to respond. When we love someone we feel the need to please them, to do things for them. I felt that need. I longed to bring others to know and to love Him, but I did not seem to be having much success. What did God want me to do? I had eighteen years to wait, then He led me to a wonderful outlet for that love and compassion.

Many people are prevented from believing because they are unable to understand God's nature. 'How could the Resurrection have taken place?' they argue. 'If God exists, why does He allow suffering?' We are conditioned to want to know all the facts, to understand. But God is supremely above us and in the spiritual dimension: we cannot expect to fully comprehend with our minds. My advice would be: 'Don't waste time trying to work it out: just be still and know that He is God.' Nothing is more worthwhile than finding Him.

As we continue on our prayerful Christian journey, through good times and bad, God does, little by little, reveal more of Himself and guides and supports us on our way. In bad, difficult and sorrowful times, we have opportunities for deepening our faith, experiencing God at a deeper level. The way of the cross was never easy but the path is well trodden by the Saints and it leads to glory.

Our Christian faith can develop from a very slender beginning – our Lord mentions 'a grain of mustard seed'. Businesses, too, often start like that, and the Loseley Dairy was no exception.

CHAPTER 10

SHALL I MAKE A CHEESE?

My father started a retail milk round with a van delivering Certified Farm Bottled Jersey milk, cream and butter before 1923. It was top quality, top price and it made a small profit at a time when many milk producers were going bankrupt. My father's first dairymaid, Nancy Bulbeck, was the shepherd's daughter, very conscientious, a great character, and Nancy remained a friend of the family, living on the Estate to the end of her life. Fifty years after Nancy started bottling milk at Loseley, her grand-daughter, Sarah, sadly suffering from spina bifida, performed the official opening of the new Dairy Plant Room, cutting the tape from her wheelchair. Happily, Sarah, although disabled, is now married with children of her own.

The round continued until 1939 when outlying customers were dropped and my father took on the deliveries himself, by day or night, when it could be fitted in, dropping some crates of Jersey milk at Guildford Station to be railed to another dairy. Maureen Benn, a friend who was on my father's wartime milk round, had been brought up on Vancouver Island, BC, and the milk was delivered by a farmer at uncertain hours. Maureen was amazed to discover that her milkmen on both sides of the Atlantic were brothers! Her Canadian milkman was my father's brother Jim who settled in Canada after the First World War. It was Jim's daughter Gee who eventually married my first business partner Mick English.

After the war we built up the Loseley retail business to around 500 gallons a day. Our first post-war dairymaid was our friend Barbara Weatherill, whose brother Bernard sometimes visited us on his two-stroke motorcycle; Bernard outgrew his two-stroke as 'Mr Speaker', now the Rt Hon. the Lord Weatherill. We engaged as rounds manager and book-keeper a conscientious, portly and good-humoured retired Major, Sid May, known to our young son as 'Big Ears', otherwise SCM. Running milk rounds is different from other businesses. Roundsmen have to get up before 6am in all weathers, they have to be efficient, polite and helpful to customers, collect the cash weekly and account for the money, and they need to be good salesmen; for all this they were not highly paid. We were lucky in having five reliable men, all different in character.

Vending machines came on the market at this period and we decided to be first in the field locally making our milk available twenty-four hours a day, with five Sankey Vendo Refrigerated Machines, in factories and outside a Guildford fish shop and the Guildway offices. We also took on a contract for cartoning and locally distributing Puritan Maid Orange Juice with Guildford Woolworths among our outlets. Like the Vendos this was, at best, marginally profitable and made life more complex.

There was keen competition between Unigate and ourselves on our rounds and we pinched quite a few customers from them; we also bought a further milk round from a local farmer. Every few months there were false rumours that Unigate were taking us over. There were no rumours in 1961 and everyone was surprised when I informed a special meeting of the roundsmen that we had accepted a very good offer from Unigate; in addition to giving us a good price for the business, they undertook to employ all our roundsmen and gave us a good contract for the supply of our bottled milk and cream. It was the skim milk arising from the cream contract that triggered an important new venture that was to transform Loseley.

On 1st April 1968 Mrs Daphne Holloway started as Farm secretary/book-keeper at Loseley. Dark and attractive, in her early 30s and recently divorced, Daphne had more besides secretarial skills: she was artistic, experienced in market research and a perfectionist. Daphne loved the countryside and old cottages: she coveted one dwelling which she had noticed in the village on her way to the interview. Daphne was thrilled when she was offered the position and that same cottage where twenty-seven years later, in appreciation of her great contribution to Loseley, she lives rent-free for life.

Daphne was to prove a second Fred Gooch, this time not flag poles but cheese. When she got down to her book-keeping, Daphne spotted that Unigate were paying us less than 1p per gallon for the skim milk. She suggested making a cottage cheese with the skim: according to Daphne I responded with enthusiasm and encouragement. Daphne took a sample of her cheese to Cranks

Health Food Shop, already customers for our organic vegetables. In Daphne's words: 'More enthusiasm, encouragement and advice.' Cranks Carnaby Street and Guildford branches became regular customers for Daphne's cheese and production had to be shifted from her cottage kitchen to the converted calf pens. The milk was soured naturally, without starters or chemicals, in ten-gallon churns, then hung from the ceiling in muslin.

Two months later Cranks yoghourt supplier let them down. 'Do you think you could make yoghourt?' asked Cranks' Director, Daphne Swann, adding: 'Our supplier in Kent would be pleased to sell you his goats.' Sue and I, Daphne and the Farm Manager, Tom Haslett, went to see the goats and decided against buying them. Then Daphne discovered that yoghourt could be produced from cow's skimmed milk. Cranks were happy with the idea and approved the sample which Daphne produced. We then set up production. The secretarial and book-keeping work was getting behind and Daphne needed to get on with packaging design and selling. We engaged a production manager, young Julie Wootton, college-trained in dairy technology, to take over production of cheese and yoghourt.

As funds were short, we had to work on a shoestring budget and went shopping for the necessary equipment at secondhand plant depots in the Hounslow area; some of the tanks and vats had come out of breweries. Soon after yoghourt production started, Sue reminded me that for a long time she had nursed the idea of making ice cream. For £40 we purchased an old ice cream machine from Mrs Sarah Lloyd-Jones, a well-known Jersey cattle breeder in Kent who was retiring.

By the end of Daphne's first year, 1968, we were in production in the old Loseley Farm buildings, with cheese, yoghourt and ice cream. Over the years many people have asked: 'Does profit sharing pay off?' In earlier days I replied: 'If you are only interested in increasing profit don't go for profit sharing. It is an attitude of mind, wanting to share, to feel in partnership with all who work in the business.' I now add that Loseley Dairy Products, our most profitable enterprise, came about through the spirit of co-partnership. Company morale and enthusiasm are assets that cannot be quantified: they are beyond price.

We managed to get planning consent for the use of the old cow sheds and ancillary buildings for manufacture of dairy products.

Unlike Guildcrete, consent was not restricted to six months but did specify: 'Not more than two people to be employed in the business.' Guildway also started in the Farmyard and at the time of our planning application for dairy products I remember the planning officer commenting: 'Out of little acorns large oak trees grow.' He was right and, like Guildway, Loseley Dairy Products was destined to outgrow both the Farmyard and our expectations, and the two employees increased to over one hundred in not many years.

We were one of the first farms to be manufacturing yoghourt and ice cream, and not many were marketing cottage cheese. In addition to these products was our cream which Loseley had been separating and selling for forty-five years. Daphne's artistic talents were given full scope in the design of the logo – Loseley House – and all the packaging. In those days, the 1970s and 1980s, the trend was for packaging to be very colourful. Daphne bucked this trend with clean white packaging, the House logo and LOSELEY in black, white and gold, elegantly projecting quality and purity. We printed the Loseley House opening season and times on the pots and cartons below the House logo. With the House open to the public, this helped to bring in more paying visitors and it stressed the point that our products are made on the Farm with the Elizabethan House which they could visit. In the surrounding parkland visitors could see the Jersey cows that produced the milk that went into the ice cream, yoghourt and cheese and they could also go on a trailer ride to see the cows being milked. Apart from boosting our Leisure Department, it helped to build a reputation.

Not as momentous as the first Guildcrete lorry in 1947, but nevertheless an exciting moment, was the arrival of our first large refrigerated van with the impressive House logo on the side. It was to be the first of a fleet of seventeen large lorries with separate freezer and refrigerated compartments.

Initially the only production worker, Julie set the highest standards, for which we were to become renowned. She worked closely with Daphne and soon we were steadily engaging more people on production, including qualified students with the National Diploma in Dairying. When Julie left to get married we again got it right in recruiting Polly Holt as Production Manager. Polly, in addition to her knowledge and enthusiasm, had the gift of getting people to enjoy working with her and morale remained high. We ensured keeping all employees well informed on the progress of the business and our plans for the future.

Manufacture of dairy products of course was discussed at a general meeting of the Loseley Co-Partnership. I pointed out that new businesses often lost money in the early years when turnover was building up. If members wished, I would be happy for the new business to be kept separate and for the Co-Partnership to receive a fair price for the milk supplied for the dairy products; alternatively, the dairy products business could be included in the Co-Partnership. We took a vote and the members were unanimously in favour of including the business. This proved a wise decision, adding several thousand pounds to the bonus over the years.

Much care and thought went into devising recipes for the ice cream and then choosing names, in which we were all involved. The resulting Old Fashioned Vanilla, Acacia Honey and Ginger, Brazilian Mocha and Montezuma Chocolate seemed good up-market names which described the product.

Selling of all the products was left to Daphne with, in early days, a little help from me. Daphne brought in Jacksons Piccadilly. I got Fortnums after a sticky interview with the chilled food buyer who said: 'I know your sort, it will be fine for a week or two, then you will let us down.' 'Give us a trial,' I urged, keeping my cool, and we were in business with Fortnum and Mason and they are still customers today. Daphne and I tackled Harrods together and walked away with a good initial order. They too are still good customers and as an extra bonus, Alastair Walker who was then Director and Harrods' Food Hall Manager, now works part-time assisting Mike in the business.

Within a few weeks we had as our regular customers Harrods, Fortnums, Jacksons Piccadilly, as well as Cranks, the leading health food restaurant. With this clientele we did not need to advertise and we were receiving an increasing number of requests from food stores, delicatessens and health food restaurants wanting to be supplied. Our success I believe stemmed from the excellence of the products and freedom from additives: we were the best. Daphne says that when visiting potential customers it never occurred to her that they would not want to stock Loseley; she even vetted prospective customers and declined to supply if she did not consider them up to standard or if they were too near an existing outlet. Those were the days!

From the beginning Daphne, Sue and I were adamant that we would set the highest standards. Jersey milk and cream were renowned for quality. Loseley House was a quality image, enhanced by Daphne's artwork. We were one of the first suppliers to claim that our products contained: 'NO artificial colouring, NO artificial flavouring, NO preservatives.' They were NATURAL. We emphasised this. We were also first to label our yoghourt as LIVE – which it is. We purchased the best, often the most expensive, ingredients and packaging and we ensured that the customer obtained excellent service. We telephoned each customer twice weekly in the mornings, peak rate, in order to take their orders for two days ahead.

People sometimes remarked that making houses and making ice cream seemed a strange mixture. My answer was that the policies of Loseley and Guildway were identical – high quality, high standards of service and conduct, teamwork and profit sharing. The technicalities were different but I was not an expert either in making houses or ice cream: I relied on technical experts in both fields.

Dairy Products was much easier to control than Guildway, much less complex and more compact, fewer product variations, fewer markets, fewer suppliers, no customer problems on mortgages or plots of land; and, above all, the dairy product was delivered complete and ready for use, whereas with Guildway the house had to be assembled by the builder.

The fleet of trucks was gradually growing and we always insisted on the drivers keeping them clean and we did not stint on repainting when vehicles started to look dingy. Daphne Holloway was utterly dedicated to maintaining quality of product and service: woe betide anyone letting down a customer. The executive who pointed out the large savings which could be made by switching from real fruit to strawberry pulp was made to wish he had kept his mouth shut! If ever a customer was let down, 'Madam', as Daphne was known to senior colleagues, was on her way the next day with goodie bag and profuse apology. To lose a customer was almost unknown. Daphne and the sales office held daily product tastings to ensure that standards were maintained.

There were minor problems, such as a change of flavour caused by something the cows had eaten in a particular field, and occasionally more serious troubles. Dairy products are vulnerable to spores from wheat and other contamination from farm crops and some of these upset the bacteria and prevent them from converting the milk into yoghourt. This did happen from time to time and on these occasions the stalwarts worked all night making a new batch of yoghourt. Besides Production Manager Polly Holt were Julia – copper-haired, lively, quick and with a sense of fun; Liz – daughter of an eminent judge, tall, fair, full of energy and a keen horsewoman; and Rosie – another real lover of animals who kept ponies, always cheerful and a real worker. Rosie's flat was next to the plant and she always extended hospitality to anyone working late or considered to be in need of refreshment.

Far worse even than the spores were the farge. We only suffered once from the farge but it was extremely serious and continued for weeks. Day after day the yoghourt would not set properly and had to be carted away to the tip. Night after night fresh batches were made. Imagine the anxiety of Polly and her stalwarts, having been up half the night, discovering as the new batch was examined that their work had to be discarded. Much more serious was the fact that our customers were not getting their Loseley yoghourt and this went on week after week. Far more damaging than the loss of sales revenue, the shops we supplied had to go to other yoghourt producers in order to satisfy their clients. We were letting down our precious customers. Fortunately our outlets were very loyal and when, thanks largely to Caroline Evans, then head of laboratory and quality control, we were at last able to supply a consistent product, our customers rejoiced and I do not think we lost any.

Growth was steady and continuous for the first few years and after the first year we were consistently profitable. To meet expansion, year by year the buildings in the old Farmyard were gradually requisitioned by Dairy Products – the cow houses, dairy and calf pens all became production areas, the workshop became the laboratory, the Dutch barn converted to two-storey packaging store. We had been so proud of our splendid modern ventilated grain store but that did not escape: the bins were demolished and the building converted from storing and drying grain to storing and refrigerating chilled products awaiting despatch. It was an impressive conversion, but it made me nostalgic and rather sad. The offices, which in 1968 had housed just Daphne and myself, were expanded to accommodate sales office, telephone sales, accounts, secretarial, computers. The shed which had been the original granary, before the building of the now-demolished grain store, had become the production and transport office. Many a sack of corn had I tipped into that little store in early years.

Most of the original equipment was simple and basic, purchased secondhand. As we expanded we needed more sophisticated plant with much higher output. The first yoghourt potting machine cost, secondhand, around £40. Less than twenty years later we had to purchase two yoghourt potters, at a total cost of £250,000. These machines operated at very high output and filled the pots, put on a sealed aluminium foil cap and then, over the foil, fitted a plastic lid and printed the date code on the pot. They then conveyed the completed pots on a conveyor; the machines were computer-controlled, with fault-finding capability and were self-cleaning. Splendid when they worked, and they usually did; but there were spells when things went very wrong and the only people who could put it right had to be summoned from Germany.

Caroline, quality control and laboratory manager, was small, dark, alert and an accomplished ballet dancer. Conscientious she had to be and she was dedicated in her persistent pursuit of the farge. Caroline's predecessor, Joan, had set up the laboratory. An experienced micro-biologist, Joan was married to Arthur Todd, the County Ministry of Agriculture Milk Officer, and had a wealth of experience behind her.

One day Joan asked to see me privately. Such requests usually indicate bad tidings and this was no exception. Kit, Joan's sister, had a baby daughter, Harriet, with a rare condition – Leigh's encephalopathy. Harriet would never be able to do anything for herself and would need constant attention. Kit, husband John and Harriet lived in the Welsh village of Llangynidr, a long way from Guildford, and Joan felt that she must give up her job to be available to help her sister with Harriet. She was very sorry at having to leave Loseley.

A few days later I went up to Great Ormond Street Children's Hospital in London and met Kit, John and Harriet for the first time. 'We know that Harriet has not long to live,' Kit said, 'but if only we could have her at home, away from hospital for her last few weeks.' We prayed together. Harriet's story was narrated by her doctor, Sandy Cavenagh, in his speech at the opening of 'Harriet's House', Tenby, West Wales, which Sue and I attended, as friends and Vice Presidents of the appeal, in May 1994. It is reproduced below with permission:

You might think that Harriet Davis' life was the ultimate tragedy. She arrived comparatively late in life to John and Kit, who by the strange quirks of fate, knew more about the development of youth and handicapped children than any of us are likely to know. For a few months all went well and then the insidious signs of Leigh's encephalopathy began. This is such a rare illness that a mere half dozen cases exist in the UK at any one time. It is due to a defect in an enzyme in the nervous system and the sufferer becomes weak and totally incapacitated. Weakness in swallowing necessitates tube feeding and poor breathing results in recurrent pneumonia, leading eventually to death.

Until Harriet, the longest survival was to the age of 7.

This was the appalling fate which befell Harriet and Kit and John. But the eventual results were not tragic at all. By some miracle, her intelligence, courage and humour were preserved to the last, and due to the super-human efforts of her parents, of the team at Nevill Hall Hospital, Abergavenny, and her many helpers at home, she survived until the age of 11. During this time her parents seldom had a night's sleep, and they provided care beyond what the best-staffed hospital in the world could offer. The result was an inspiration to her family and friends and to all who came in touch with her.

And it did not end there. By their efforts in fund-raising John and Kit have sent £70,000 to the Research Trust for Metabolic Diseases in Children and £130,000 towards the Harriet Davis Seaside Holiday Trust, providing many families with similar problems with rest and recuperation in the specially equipped seaside holiday home.

I suspect we should judge the value of a life not by its length, but by the amount of love it generates. In those terms Harriet was a centenarian. Her name will remain in perpetuity – or at least as long as Tenby stands – and her illness and life have made at least one not very Christian practitioner ponder anew the meaning of immortality.

The opening was performed by the Rt Revd Dewi Bridges, Bishop of Swansea, who had confirmed Harriet, describing this as the most moving event of his life. For Sue and I it was a great privilege to have known Harriet and the family, and that was thanks to Joan Todd giving me notice terminating her employment with Dairy Products at Loseley. It is to Dairy Products that we must now return.

CHAPTER 11

SMALL WAS BEAUTIFUL

In 1978 Mike returned home as an active Farming Partner, after three years at the Royal Agricultural College, Cirencester, followed by practical experience on the Northumberland farms of Nigel, now Lord Vinson. Dairy Products had now become by far the most profitable and fastest growing Loseley Department, taking most of our management time, including David Cripps the Farm Manager. In 1982 Mike, as Managing Partner, took over responsibility for Dairy Products within the Partnership and I remained Chairman.

Loseley Dairy Products had built up a splendid image, morale was high and sales continued to grow. Costs were growing too: new buildings, new plant, new people. We were caught in the spiral and had to continue increasing sales to keep up with costs.

We were aware of changes in the market: we were supplying up-market grocers, delicatessens, health food stores and health restaurants. Year by year the supermarkets, in Daphne's vocabulary 'the dreaded supermarkets', were claiming an increasing share of the food market and if our expansion was to continue we had to revise our attitude to these outlets. It was an agonising decision, particularly for Daphne, so loyal to her independent customers, so jealous of our reputation. If Loseley was on sale in cut-price supermarkets it would undercut our loyal independent outlets and down-grade our image, but if we declined to supply them our sales would steadily fall.

Eventually and reluctantly Daphne agreed, although fretting that the supermarkets diminished our 'top of the market' position, for which we had all worked so long and so hard. She also resented waiting in line with all the other reps for the young and powerful buyer's favours. Loseley did not appear in all the supermarkets: although some of them coveted the Loseley image, they would only take our product on their heavily discounted terms. The supermarkets' requirements were very precise; once a box of ice cream on a delivery was found to be 1 per cent over the specified temperature and the whole consignment was rejected. Understandably, there were also tight specifications regarding buildings and production facilities; by then we had built our new plant room: the inspectors would not have appreciated some of the old converted cow sheds!

The supermarket buyers were a different breed from the independents, hard-headed professionals and in a strong position because of their volume business. There were queues of would-be suppliers knocking on their doors and they could afford to be tough: their jobs depended on it. When Mike announced that Sainsbury had become our largest customer, Sue was unimpressed. Since Sainsbury first opened on Good Friday many years ago, Sue warned that if they persisted she would never use Sainsbury again and she holds to that. If more people had followed Sue's example we might have succeeded in keeping Sunday special.

Like Guildway, Loseley had a notional 'club' embracing customers, suppliers and consultants, regarding them as part of the team and as friends. Daphne counted as personal friends most of our independent customers. David and Kay Canter and Daphne Swann, the Directors of our first customer Cranks, were personal friends of ours and shared our convictions on organic farming and that money and maximum profit are not the most important things in life. Sadly David Canter died in his 50s and it was at his funeral that Sue and I met Sir Ronald Harris, a charming and very talented Christian, who had had a distinguished career which included holding the offices of Private Secretary to the Secretary of the War Cabinet and finally as First Church Commissioner in which he greatly increased the Church's revenue. It was Ronald who introduced us to Bishop Morris Maddocks, leading to my official entry to the Christian Healing Ministry. That is another chapter but it is a strange fact that two people met by chance at funerals became very significant on my Christian journey.

Through service, loyalty and Daphne's attentions, the independent shops survived the experience of seeing Loseley products in supermarkets at discounted prices, and most of the individual customers continued their patronage, being prepared to pay a little more for the helpful service and atmosphere of the independent outlets. For many years we supplied British Airways with bombes for first-class long-haul flights. Every three months we had to develop a new bombe: the BA catering team led by Kurt Hafner knew what they wanted and Daphne and her team worked until they met the specification and by then it was time to start development on the next bombe.

It was on honeymoon in Ireland in 1948 that I had the idea of Customer Days and the following summer we invited all our milk customers to tea on the Loseley lawn and this became an annual event. I have a photograph of one of these early occasions, with cloth caps much in evidence. With Dairy Products we continued Customer Days, inviting to our Garden Party our shop-keeper customers from Harrods to the village shop. They toured the House and Garden, saw the cows milked and walked round the factory which, being Sunday, was not operating. Then strawberry and cream tea in the Marquee or Barn and displays and tastings of new products and the opportunity for our customers to comment and give their suggestions. There were 800 guests in later years on Customer Day and on the previous day, Saturday, we held the Loseley and Guildway Staff and Pensioners Garden Party, so by Sunday evening our right hands had been much shaken and squeezed. There was a lot of work involved as well as some expense, but it was well worthwhile, rewarding loyalty and building friendships.

More suspect to me is the cost of Press advertising and I would not sanction it. We spent money on service, including peak time telephoning for orders, kept the vehicles smart and invested in good packaging. We had an enviable reputation, built on a shoestring and on merit, not hype. Many of our competitors were cash-rich public companies and any advertising we might have done would have been dwarfed and swamped by our competitors. In later years we did employ Dairy Products sales representatives to keep in touch with customers and to find new ones. Among the sales force was a lovely girl, Mrs Diana Brewster, fair, lively, sensitive and with a beautiful singing voice. Very sadly, Diana developed cancer. She joined the Loseley Christian Cancer Centre as well as being in the care of the medics. She seemed to be making good progress but, after a family holiday on the Greek islands, Diana's health rapidly deteriorated and she died, leaving her husband Martin to bring up two-year-old Hannah.

The longest-serving salesman is John Blaney, a bright and cheerful person, always ready with a quip. Despite the lighthearted approach, John is a conscientious and successful salesman with an unusual sideline: he is an accomplished butter sculptor and produced for Harrods a wonderful pair of green wellies made from butter.

Although we did not advertise, we were aware of the importance of PR and members of the Press were members of 'the club'. Dairy Products had an unpleasant experience with the Press. A death had occurred due to someone eating hazelnut yoghourt. It was not Loseley yoghourt and we did not use product containing the fatal ingredient but two days later *Today* newspaper published a photograph of Loseley hazelnut yoghourt on the shelves of a store above the bold headline 'Killer Yoghourt Still On Sale'. Understandably our hazelnut yoghourt sales plummeted and never completely recovered. Many innocent people have been more deeply hurt by the irresponsibility of the Gutter Press. As Guildway were to learn, TV also is not blameless in this respect.

There was a time in Guildway's history when things were going well and when we were the acknowledged leaders in the timber-frame housing field. It was then that letters started arriving: 'We are interested in the possibility of acquiring your business.' Now Loseley Dairy Products were getting similar approaches which received a polite but firm 'No.' Then came a letter from Kraft. Mike, now managing the business, with myself as Chairman, suggested: 'No harm in seeing what sort of figure they have in mind.' I agreed. Well done Mike! I would not have considered selling, although I remembered the lost opportunities for selling Guildway. It made sense to sell at the top and margins were beginning to shrink with more business going through the 'dreaded' supermarkets, less through independents. Competition was steadily increasing, partly from other farmers recognising our success and wanting to join in on the action.

We had visits from members of the aristocracy wanting to find out how we did it, including two Marquises, a Duchess and a number of Peers. A few went ahead with manufacturing, with varying degrees of success. Many of the farmer competitors gave up because of technical problems, or discovering that becoming a manufacturer was not as easy as it looked and it was better to stick to farming, the job they knew. One of our customers, Jacksons Piccadilly, increased their cream order, explaining that their previous supplier, a Peer of the Realm, arranged for deliveries by his wife, when she happened to be passing: sometimes this was when the store was closed and the consignment of cream was left on the doorstep to be discovered and brought in when the store opened. I happened to meet the Peer some time later and he verified the story.

More serious was the competition from large public companies and European producers of yoghourt. Another factor was capital. Although we were making good profits, the bank overdraft was rising because of the expenditure needed for new buildings and plant, to keep pace with expansion and to meet the rigorous requirements of the supermarkets.

Selling a business was a new situation for us and we needed professional advice on the worth of our company; a prospectus had to be prepared, negotiations conducted. Mike and I went up for a meeting with our accountants in their smart new City offices, fully air-conditioned, no windows. Reception area staffed by heavily made-up young women wearing bow ties and pink jackets, more like a night club than an accountancy firm and a far cry from the Victorian offices and the clanging metal lift gates of chartered accountants Limebeer and Company, when I went for that 'non-liquidation' meeting in 1956. Now we had come to discuss not liquidation but the sale of a successful company. How pleased Gillie Potier, Meryn Lewis and John Owers would have been . . . One so often thinks of them, always with gratitude. They had really cared about our businesses: Meryn certainly worried about them more than I did. Advisers in those days did not regard their clients as 'profit centres'.

After a few meetings our new London accountants rightly decided that it was appropriate to transfer us to their provincial office which dealt with farms and estates and at more affordable rates. We did not miss leaving the night club ladies and at the new office the staff were most helpful and efficient.

Mike, Sue, Daphne and I had some interesting meetings with Kraft directors at their Cheltenham offices and at Loseley, and we visited one of their factories producing sausage rolls, but eventually negotiations stalled. Mike and I had cordial meetings and visits with the HP Bulmer Board of Hereford, a very well-run company, profit sharing and, like Loseley, members of the Industrial Participation Association, as the Industrial Co-Partnership Association is now called. Going round the Bulmer plant with the chairman and production director one noticed a difference: the directors took an interest in the people in the factory and enquired of one of them about his health problems. Typical of a Co-Partnership firm.

Booker was a company unknown to us. They were big in food distribution, farm management, tree nurseries, forestry, turkey breeding in the USA, salmon farming and processing in Scotland and Canada, and mushrooms. Booker also own the Agatha Christie copyright and are probably best known as sponsors of the annual Booker Literary Prize. They showed interest in Loseley and Mike and I had a meeting with the Managing Director, Jonathan Taylor. Afterwards a main Board Director, Antony Haynes, came to hold further discussions. Fortunately I am very seldom unwell but on that day I had flu and a high temperature. I left the proceedings to Mike, making a brief unscheduled appearance in my dressing gown to meet Antony in the Great Hall, and shortly afterwards I lunched with him at the Booker headquarters at Portland House, Stag Place. Antony's office on the fourteenth floor overlooks the gardens of Buckingham Palace, with a view at Garden Party time of the guests eating their Loseley ice cream. We got on well and soon afterwards four directors came down and went round the plant and the Farm.

Booker commissioned market research in the supermarkets and asked the views of customers about Loseley. The report on this was almost embarrassingly good – Loseley was conceived as being very sound, good and pure, high standards, healthy, a family business, Elizabethan home, made-on-the-farm. Idyllic. Loseley was undoubtedly best and Booker were impressed.

At the negotiation stage, at Mike's suggestion, we employed Hoare Govett to act for us. Mike and I had a number of interesting meetings at the offices of Hoare Govett in the fascinating new Broadgate development and here the hard bargaining took place with Antony Haynes. We got to the point where neither side was prepared to give ground. I remember saying to Antony: 'I am very sorry that we have wasted your time.' Antony, with his usual charm, assured us that the time was not wasted. Next day Richard Wilson of Hoare Govett rang to say that negotiations were continuing, that Booker definitely wanted to buy our business and were proposing a compromise solution which he thought would be acceptable. We eventually agreed and the deal was done.

Two years earlier we had formed Dairy Products into a separate company, Loseley Dairy Products Limited. Mike was Managing

Director, myself Chairman, Daphne Holloway Sales Director, Adrian Abbott Accountant and Financial Director, with Sue and Glye Hodson Non-Executive Directors.

The legal business of the deal was complex and long-winded: the lawyers on both sides had a bonanza. Fax at that time was relatively new and we were loaned a portable fax machine to assist communications. The final signing took place at Portland House, attended by Sue, Mike and I, Daphne Holloway as Trustee of Loseley and Guildway Charitable Trust, David Turner the Booker Finance Director and our respective lawyers.

Our two charities had no tax to pay on their proceeds and it was a great satisfaction to me that they were now well funded. The family were able to make a substantial endowment for the Loseley House Maintenance Fund and for almost the first time since 1946 we were no longer overdrawn at the bank. At last I could feel that Loseley was secure for my lifetime, yet there were dangers in the removal of the survival challenge and we still needed to control expenditure.

Outwardly the sale to Booker did not constitute a significant change in the dairy business, but in fact it was very different. Although the plant, offices and staff were the same, the family, although running the business day-to-day, was no longer in control. When a large public company takes over a small family business the policy for that business is nearly always rapid growth. With a small family business finance has to be tightly controlled and expenditure kept down but now Booker were aiming at rapid expansion, and capital for them was not a problem.

Daphne Holloway retired in April 1989 and I appointed her Life President of Loseley Dairy Products Limited. We recruited, through an expensive head-hunter, a Sales Director who was ambitious and energetic. In order to get volume business he dedicated himself to getting big orders from supermarkets, particularly 'own label', and Daphne's precious independents had to take second place. Inevitably on occasion independent shops received incomplete deliveries because Sainsbury had to have priority on supplies and our independent customers soon realised that Loseley had changed. There did not seem to be the same personal caring, and the era of Daphne and her goodie bags was no more.

Daphne's successor, the new Sales Director, put up a strong case for building a new ice cream factory at Alton, twenty miles from Loseley. He assured Booker and the Loseley Dairy Products Board that he could obtain large orders from the supermarkets, particularly Sainsbury, for 'own label' ice cream but that we would not get the orders without building a new factory. Sue and I were away when the Board visited the proposed factory at Alton but we went over the following week with Daphne Holloway. We did not like it. Outside space was very restricted, unlike Loseley, with room for only one large vehicle, and we were reprimanded for walking along the service road at the side of the Alton factory: we were trespassing, it was not our road.

Our really decisive 'No' vote came from the horrific and evil smell. Something in the nature of burning plastic, it was really sinister and unhealthy and emanated from the next-door factory. If the Sainsbury inspectors had smelt that, they would certainly have black-listed the factory. Into my mind that evening came the memory of the burglar alarm going off, warning that Kelly was trying to steal Guildway. Now the warning was that the Alton factory was a 'bad smell'. The burglar alarm never again behaved as it did when it warned me of Kelly, and that terrible Alton smell apparently never surfaced again. If I had been in control, that would have been the end of the Alton factory.

Sue and I voted against Alton but the project went ahead. The conversion of the factory was efficiently carried out and on time. It was a lovely 'state of the art' ice cream production unit, which cost around £2 million. We had a grand opening with the Press and local dignitaries invited and I arranged for Daphne Holloway, as Life President of the company, to unveil the plaque. There were fascinating machines, long conveyors, spiral freezers, everywhere machines doing jobs previously performed by human beings – 'look no hands!' Empty tubs revolved in cages, dropped in the right spot for filling and lidding, then up the spiral to be frozen and down again to the packaging conveyors.

Fascinating and most impressive it certainly was, but the orders in the promised volume failed to materialise. Then the recession and a plunge into losses. On my retirement Mike succeeded me as Chairman. I had been due to retire when we sold the business but at Antony's insistence I agreed to continue for two years but declined to accept a salary. I later found out how much Mike was paid for the job and realised how stupid I had been. In the old days I had always said: 'If I have a roof over my head, produce to eat and petrol in my car, that's all I need.' I was a dedicated amateur. A professional Managing Director was now recruited.

Board meetings continued to be held monthly in the Drawing Room at Loseley House and we entertained the Board to lunch in the Dining Room. Two Booker directors sat on the Board and they were charming, courteous and helpful with many sound ideas. Loseley was different from any company they had ever known and I think they enjoyed the experience and certainly we enjoyed their company and appreciated their experience. There was probably more variety at Loseley than at Booker's Portland House Headquarters.

One Board meeting coincided with the second Great Storm when many trees were lost. The thick walls and double-glazing in the Drawing Room dampened the sound and it was an eerie sight to see through the windows the trees straining, bending before the frenzied gale, leaves, twigs, branches torn off. On the day of another Board meeting I had to be on duty as Vice Lord Lieutenant at a Royal visit in the county immediately following the meeting, and I chaired the meeting booted and spurred, in uniform.

Experienced, hard-headed, intelligent and sound as they were, the Booker directors, like us, hoped that somehow the Loseley mystique would see the company through, but very sadly it did not. Eventually Booker sold the ice-cream business and the Alton factory, together with the name Loseley Dairy Ice Cream Limited, to a relatively new and successful ice-cream company. The chilled products business, which remained on the Loseley site, was sold to Tim Hennecker-Parker who had sold his previous dairy products business in East Anglia. His firm, now named Loseley Chilled Products Limited, took over the Dairy Products plant and buildings in the old Farmyard as tenants of Loseley.

A family connection is maintained with Mike as a Non-Executive Director, and with overheads slashed they are doing quite well. The company uses our Loseley Jersey milk and carries our name, and it is important to us that the quality standards are maintained.

Booker were very fair with us and, as far as I am aware, they never tried to put the blame on the family. The recession came at the worst possible time for them. Loseley was best and among the most expensive and in times of recession people trade down. When Booker took over, there was inevitably priority for rapid growth and that dictated priority to supermarkets. Coupled with

Daphne's retirement, the effect on the higher margin business with the independents was significant. The Loseley image had been built up on the small, wholesome, family business and products made-on-the-farm. Having sold the business to a large public company, with our ice cream now produced on the Alton Trading Estate, we could no longer be true to our image.

What if we had remained independent? We would have needed to raise capital, possibly obtaining a USM listing. We would have been severely dented by the recession, but without the Alton factory overheads would have been a lesser millstone. It was to Mike's credit that we decided to sell the business and for us that was the right decision. I have lived dangerously for most of my forty years in business and now, ten years past official retirement age, I'd plump for safety.

Loseley House is the logo appearing on all Loseley dairy products. The House itself forms part of another business, a business that is not for sale.

CHAPTER 12

OPEN TO THE PUBLIC

It was a tremendous feat of Sue's, to have got the House from its dereliction in 1946 to be ready for public viewing in 1950. We opened four afternoons a week from June until 30th September at two shillings a head. I wish that we had taken photographs in the early days to compare with the present but we were too busy and the House too derelict and depressing. The unavoidable neglect of the war years, damp coming through broken windows, lack of heating, all had taken their toll. Sue always disclaims any credit: 'All my helpers . . .' She had two stalwart part-timers: Mrs Colin Reeves (Joyce), whose husband was tractor driver foreman on the Farm, and her sister, Mrs Tom Reeve (Phyl), whose husband was head gardener. Phyl Reeve specially remembers the cold in winter, cleaning and polishing in her warmest clothes, topped with overcoat, gloves and scarves. Mrs Colin had been trained as a housemaid under a very demanding first employer. The lady set traps to catch her out, such as putting dirt underneath the edge of the carpet and Joyce was severely reprimanded if she failed to spot it. Sue was too busy and too appreciative of getting help to want to set traps and there was enough dirt without having to plant any.

The rooms that we opened to the public were the Great Hall, Library, Drawing Room and the four West Wing Bedrooms. As well as cleaning and polishing the floors and the panelling in all the rooms and passages, there was the furniture to put in order, including protection from furniture beetle and much polishing. Chalk chimneypieces needed much scrubbing and the ironwork in fireplaces had to be wire-brushed before black-leading and polishing. Apart from the cleaning and polishing, for Sue there were the windows on three floors to be opened when the weather was dry and shut at the end of the day or when it rained. There were moths in curtains, sometimes birds trapped in rooms, always the need to look for tell-tale little heaps of furniture beetle borings; there were flowers to be picked and arranged in all the rooms and then, probably Sue's favourite duty in the House, the clocks in every room, all going and keeping correct time. So much dedicated effort.

We had a simple guide-book printed which sold at 1s 6d. We advertised in the local press and we must have done some PR, for the *Daily Mail* sent a photographer to photograph Sue and me fixing a sign in front of the House. The photograph was duly published, captioned 'Loseley House Opens Up'. I remember that our main concern was to get our Labrador included in the picture and we remonstrated that the place chosen by the photographer was nowhere near where the sign was actually going. We were still at the beginning of our learning curve on PR and the ways of the Press, but we did learn and we have had many good write-ups over the years on the House, Guildway and Dairy Products, including an unsolicited family feature in *Hello!* magazine in October 1994 which included: 'The Chapel is the vital part of the soul of the House.'

Appropriately, visitors enter through the inner door of the Entrance Hall under an archway inscribed *Invidiae claudor, pateo sed semper amico* – 'I am shut to envy but always open to a friend'. George Neville, retired butler, and Miss Coltham, my old Nanny, took turns to act as guide. Nanny had many charges after handing me over but I was fortunate in remaining her favourite. Mr and Mrs Neville occupied the main lodge and on retirement we arranged for Nanny to have a bed-sitter in the building. She guarded the lodge-gate with great tenacity and refused entry to any who she felt unworthy and especially to any lorries which were likely to further enlarge the pot-holes. Nanny was touchingly loyal: the view from her window stretched beyond the drive gates to the Guildway factory and Nanny counted the lorries that went out each day and rejoiced for us on the good days. When we had cut hay and during harvest, being superstitious, she would never clean her windows as she did not want to make it rain! I shall always be grateful to her for her loyalty and affection, not only in my early years but to the end of her life.

As the House guide, Nanny was not quite in her element but would always have a go to help out. At that time there was a large picture on the staircase, known as 'The Allegorical Picture'. Nanny passed it by with the comment: 'That's the Archipelago Picture' and she got away with it without any queries or questions: she would have had a harder time with today's public. In the early 1950s there were not many Houses open to the public; our visitors felt it a privilege to be admitted and were not over-demanding.

I occasionally received correspondence from visitors. One letter contained complex queries about the coats of arms on the Drawing Room chimneypiece. Being desperately busy with Guildcrete and the Farm and knowing nothing about heraldry, I put the letter in the pending tray, hoping to think of someone who might know the answers. Two weeks later a telegram arrived: 'You are obviously offended by my letter. Kindly consider it withdrawn.' I telegraphed back: 'Not offended, merely baffled by heraldry.' All was well and eventually the required information was despatched. We get regular requests for information on past members of the family, some from strangers who think they might be related to us and these tend to go into that pending tray. I have stated on occasion that I knew more about my cows' pedigrees than my own, and the cows' pedigrees were more important, which genetically is a fact. Our main manuscripts are on permanent loan to the Surrey Record Office in the Guildford Muniment Room and the staff are always helpful. There must be a vast number of theses written on Sir William More, judging by all the people writing to us requesting information on him.

That first year we had around a thousand visitors, but the decision to get the House in order and open to the public was much more significant than we realised at the time. The House was now transformed from a slumbering grubby geriatric, unkempt, to a beautiful much-loved creature, friendly, steeped in peace, that people loved to visit. There was no going back. Forty years on, numbers round the House were only about ten thousand but total visitors to Loseley including grounds and events are around a hundred thousand.

For the second season we recruited a professional guide and through the years, as numbers increased, we took on more guides; we now have eighteen experienced guides available, but only four and a door-keeper are on duty at the same time. Our first guide was a retired officer, Major Taylor, inexperienced in guiding but well informed, friendly and patient. On his retirement Miss Mollie Ayre-Smith took over as chief guide. She was very authoritative and had served in the WRAF, so I christened her the 'Wing Commander'. Mollie was an excellent organiser as well as being knowledgeable. We are fortunate with our guides: they are all keen and learn a little more each year from the visitors. There are many top specialists among the visitors – specialists in decorative arts, in furniture of the sixteenth, seventeenth and eighteenth centuries, specialists in porcelain, in native weapons, Elizabethan lifestyle, in all types and periods of painting.

Experts do not always agree and are not always right. One who was right is Sir Roy Strong. On visiting him one day in London we mentioned that we had a portrait of Queen Elizabeth by Zuchero. 'I bet it isn't,' replied Sir Roy. 'Zuchero would have had to have lived two hundred years to have painted all the pictures of Queen Elizabeth attributed to him.' Roy Strong came to lunch at Loseley. 'Is that Queen Elizabeth by Zuchero?' I challenged as he stood before the portrait. 'It certainly isn't Zuchero and I very much doubt if it is Queen Elizabeth either!' In fact we discovered that Sir Roy was absolutely right and the portrait has been removed from the Great Hall. It is recorded in my parents' book on the Loseley paintings as being 'Queen Elizabeth by Zuchero'.

Most of the experts are very helpful. The tapestry in the Queen's Room is Mortlake. We knew that one of the characters was King David, for his name is on his garter. Some years later a young girl spotted a very faint 'Abigail' on the sleeve of the lady with David. Then one day a visitor gave us, literally, chapter and verse for the scene: 1 Samuel 25. I happened to be taking that party round. 'I am most impressed,' I told the visitor. 'It's my job,' he replied. 'I'm secretary of the Bible Society!' Our guides are very conscientious and every season many people take the trouble to write in appreciation. We occasionally receive complaints but very seldom about the guides.

Over the years the House tours have little changed but more facilities and attractions have been added. Within a few years Sue said: 'We really should provide tea for the visitors.' So we did. At first it was very simple – a cuppa with scone, cream and strawberry jam or cake, served through the Scullery window, eaten at picnic tables in the Courtyard. For booked coach parties we used the Billiard Room. The Billiard Room before the war became the Gun Room, then, in our day, Mike's Play Room, then a spell as an office and at this time it made an excellent Tea Room for booked coach parties. Now it is a Games Room for the grandchildren: Loseley is very adaptable.

By chance I provided three successive tea ladies – Joan Newman and her successor Nancy Smith arrived via Guildway as already described and their scones and cakes were much appreciated by the visitors. Anne Matthews, the third tea lady recruited by me came in through a prayer group to which we both belonged and she also was a superb cook. Following the termination of an unhappy marriage, Anne was bringing up her two children on her own, doing some private catering and finding time to assist alcoholics through AA. Over the years Anne lovingly assisted a number of my friends, not alcoholics, including my half-sister at a critical time of ill health.

Although not actually tea ladies, two other delightful helpers were recruited for Loseley rather in the manner of Joan and Cyril Newman. Sue and I stayed for two nights at a very pleasant hotel in the wilds of Wales. Jane Allison, the owner/manager, was a lovely person: bright, efficient, friendly. Her husband, partner in the hotel, was an ex-RAF pilot who longed to get back to flying. When we left we said to Jane, as I had said to the Newmans years before: 'If ever you give up this hotel, do let us know.'

A few years later Jane telephoned to ask if we would be at home the next weekend when she and her friend, Jenny, planned to visit the Loseley Craft Fair. They came and lunched with us. Jenny was the wife of another ex-RAF pilot. Jane and Richard had sold the hotel and were living near Gatwick where Richard and Jenny's husband, Frank, were based as pilots. Jane and Jenny were lively yet sensitive and we took to them from the start. At the time Sue had a big problem. The visitor season was just starting and her splendid and only full-time help in the House, Minh Phuong from Vietnam, was leaving in a week with her family for America, summoned by Minh's father-in-law who was in poor health. Minh dreaded the thought of not returning to Loseley, but expected to be away for some years. 'Don't worry, we'll help you,' said Jane and Jenny to Sue. That season those girls really saved the situation. They came over three or four days a week from Gatwick, cleaned, cooked, did anything needed, and they worked so fast that they often had time over to help with the flower borders. They tackled everything with apparent joy, reminding us of those early days, when we all worked and laughed together, Sue and Donny, John, Barbara . . .

With the advent of Loseley Dairy Products in 1968 the time was ripe for a Loseley Shop. The old Game Larder was ideal, situated in the Courtyard near the teas and the public lavatories.

I remember the Game Larder before the war: pheasants, partridges and rabbits hung from hooks and nails in the ceiling timbers. My father sometimes cured bacon and hams there and I recollect long sessions with brine and rubbing and turning. In my school days the Game Larder bored me; now it was exciting as we transformed the great slate slabs into sales counters. In addition to ice cream, cream, yoghourt and cheese, we sold John Newman's scones and cakes and Jersey cattle tea-towels.

Our first shopkeeper was Joan's husband Cyril, very much at home serving the public again behind the counter rather than, as landlord, behind the bar. Daphne Holloway took a deep interest and her artistic eye was a great help in laying out the Shop. We then took on the lease of a shop in Crown Court, Godalming. This was expertly managed by Mrs Josie Kane, wife of one of our Guildway directors, but the higher overheads of a town shop were not matched by the anticipated growth in turnover and we relinquished the lease after two years. Meanwhile the Game Larder Shop prospered and was destined to move, with the teas, to larger accommodation.

Running a small shop can be a very rewarding occupation. We have been very fortunate in our shop managers. Sue's sister, Donny, really did talk people into buying: 'Have you tried this? – it really is delicious. People keep coming back for more.' She is so conscientious that she will not allow Sue or me to help in the Shop: 'No I'm fine thank you, I know how I want things.' Another stalwart shop manager has been Sylvia Haslett, for many years my secretary at Guildway. Sylvia originated the Loseley Christmas Fair which she runs very successfully in the Barn each year, with an additional marquee for charities.

With the passing of the years, people became more demanding and teas 'through the window' were not pukka enough. By now we were taking the public seriously and Fred Gooch, recently retired from Guildway and now Life President, suggested moving from an outlying farm a disused seventeenth-century tithe barn, dilapidated to the point of partial collapse. Fred is a Norfolk man with a creative imagination and the determination to make dreams come true. An awesome project, but with Fred it would succeed. We decided to site it on the west side of the lawn and planning consent was obtained. Fred numbered the timbers in the Barn with dymo-labels and made detailed plans of the building.

Tile by tile, piece by piece, the barn was taken down at Conduit Farm and hauled to the edge of our lawn. Then piece by piece and tile by tile it was re-erected. The building was 20ft wide with a 10ft lean-to along the side for kitchen, stores and shop. When half complete I decided that it was not big enough – I wanted another 40ft, to make the barn 100ft long. We found the extra barn. Years ago Marley Tile Company had bought an outlying farmstead for expansion of their concrete factory: now they wanted to get rid of the tithe barn on the site. Planning consent for the barn to be taken down was eventually granted on condition that the building was re-erected at Loseley.

We were given the barn free of charge, Loseley to dismantle and remove it. We added a lean-to south room, as private dining room or seminar room, built from green oak felled by the great winds of October 1987, sawn on the Loseley bandsaw. Fred and Larry, retired maintenance foreman, laid the floor in the whole 2,000 sq. ft barn from Loseley oak strips. The barn has a lovely atmosphere, aged, with a mellow dignity yet warm and friendly. It was honoured in 1991 with an Award in the CLA Farm Buildings Competition.

The use of Guildway for business entertaining and promotion is not new. My company, Guildway Limited, had made good use of Loseley facilities for many years. I often brought Guildway customers, contacts and suppliers back to Loseley for lunch. Most were appreciative and found it a change from pubs and restaurants. The annual Sales Conference had been held in the Great Hall and in the Billiard Room for a number of years. On one occasion our guest speaker was a senior member from a well-known sales training company. He had just commenced his talk when the door opened and a little man burst into the room. Wearing an old jacket and corduroy trousers, rather bedraggled, his elderly face weather-beaten and lined; his eyes glared and he was very angry.

'Someone in here is not a gentleman,' he yelled. 'Someone see simple working man on bicycle, don't care, drive fast through puddles, nearly knock me off, cover me with mud and water . . . You think me just common working man. What you think you are?'

The stream of invective paused, the glaring eyes had recognised the quarry – the guest speaker, standing right ahead of him: 'It's YOU,' he screamed. The poor speaker was so shaken and embarrassed that he could not even gasp 'Sorry'. He stood there silent, consumed with embarrassment and possibly shame. I managed to pacify Rudi, for he it was, and the Sales Conference got under way again; but it was Rudi who stole the show.

Rudi was a real character. He was Lithuanian and claimed to have served in three armies during the war, ending up as a PoW in England. He had lost touch with his family and believed they were all dead. Rudi was a self-taught craftsman as stone mason, drain layer, cobblestone layer, rustic wood-worker. 'In my country we are poor, if you want something – shoes, furniture, whatever – you make it.' Anything Rudi made was well made. After many narrow escapes, Rudi was eventually knocked down by a car when returning from the pub; he was nearly eighty. The world is poorer without him but Rudi leaves behind many memorials: walls, seats, barbecue, paving, cobbles.

Our Board meetings were sometimes held at Loseley in the Great Hall, with lunch in the Dining Room. Jeff Chittle, our lively Production Director, had been a fleet air arm pilot during the war. One day when his plate of meat was put before him Jeff became transfixed; it was not the food that excited him but the cook who was serving it. Jeff recognised her, for he had been to see her four nights running at the Liverpool Adelphi Theatre during the war. On those occasions she removed her clothes, for this was Phyllis Dixie, the celebrated 'stripper' who at one time leased the Haymarket Theatre. Phyllis Dixie had fallen on hard times and she was now helping Sue. She was a good cook and so elegant, it was a joy to watch Phyllis even removing the joint from the oven; but there was no cabaret to follow the meal.

Important among our charity events is the annual Queen Elizabeth's Foundation for Disabled People Classic Car Show. Fred Gooch, for many years a member of the Council and Advisory Committee of this splendid Charity, chaired the first Classic Car Show in 1991. Sadly, that Saturday turned out to be the wettest day of the summer and the Sunday was showery. People understandably did not pour in by the thousand but in succeeding years the QEF Classic Car Show has become increasingly popular and successful.

Loseley Farm Tours is an important section of Loseley Leisure Department, never intended as a money-making operation, although a charge is made to cover the operating costs. This educational activity is very popular with children and we are now getting some of our earlier schoolchildren visitors returning as mums bringing their own children on the tour. Farm tours were in fact started to try and help our friend, John Charlton, who did a spell at Loseley soon after the war. After a two-year course at Agricultural College John had taken on the tenancy of a Loseley smallholding. He had worked hard but unfortunately contracted lung problems and had to give up farming. Afterwards John got married and built up a good wine business from his home at Thame. Then, sadly, his wife moved out and he had to sell up. We needed to find John a job, somewhere to live and, hopefully, a wife: I had the plan which might have provided all three: it nearly did!

At the time another marriage had sadly come to an end, the husband having gone off leaving his loving, hard-working wife of twenty-five years and their children. I knew that John and this newly deserted wife had long ago been quite fond of one another and it seemed sensible to offer John a job and suggest that accommodation might be available: but what job? John had farming experience and occasionally I had had to spend precious time taking a school party or overseas visitors round the Farm. If we had someone to do this full-time, we might build farm tours into something worthwhile.

John did not take much persuading and my selected landlady, a kind and most unselfish person of impeccable character, offered him separate accommodation in her spacious house. John made an inauspicious start by overturning a trailer-load of children in a ditch. Fortunately there was only one casualty, a 7-year-old girl who suffered a broken leg. She was very brave, the parents understanding and the insurance company paid up. After that we changed the route and used smaller trailers, eventually building special ones. The tractor and trailer went from the House and across fields to Orange Court Farm.

Having seen viewing galleries in milking parlours in the USA, we incorporated this feature in our new parlour. After watching the milking, the visitors saw the calves and, returning through the fields, John would tell them about livestock on view and the names of trees and birds. Once even a snake showed up but Sue and I felt we needed a greater variety of farm animals.

At that point we received another significant telephone call, this time from a lady called Chloe, whose husband had left. Chloe, with a large collection of rare breeds, including thirty breeds of sheep, several pigs, a variety of poultry from bantams to geese, turkeys and peacocks, had to move out. She urgently needed a house, five-acre field and buildings for her livestock. Sue and I went over to see Chloe and the animals. Chloe, short, wiry and very active, took us round. We liked her and obviously she was very fond of the animals: they were well kept. We wanted to help, we needed the livestock and we had a field at Orange Court for the animals, and for Chloe the field contained a Guildway bungalow which was becoming vacant the next month. Chloe and her menagerie moved in. There were some special characters, such as Diana the ewe who shook hands, and an enormous turkey called Marmalade who was very friendly. The ugliest and among the most popular animals were the Vietnamese pot-bellied pigs, but baby pigs of all breeds are irresistible.

A number of rare breeds are already extinct and it is only through the dedicated work of the Rare Breeds Society and its members like Chloe that the decline is being halted. Apart from the need for preservation for historical reasons, there is more flavour in the meat of rare breeds than in the modern breeds specially developed for rapid growth and efficient food conversion.

John, as the Farm Guide, was now in his element. He steadily built up the numbers of children, mostly school parties, and the farm tours became very popular. After two seasons it became clear to John that his 'intended' did not intend to regard him as more than a good friend and he moved on. It is a fact of life that often when you work hard for something to happen it doesn't, but something else does happen. By the time John left, the farm tours had become so popular that we had to engage a new warden. I took on a farmer's daughter from Northumberland, not this time as a marriage bureau, but for the Leisure job. Sarah Westmacott had been in charge of the sheep at home, was good on a horse and fond of animals and the countryside. She wanted a job for the summer months: in October she was going to work for a spell in Australia, where she had relations.

Sarah had a successful season with the children and the animals. On her way back from Australia she called at Hong Kong where she met up again with our son Mike and they got engaged somewhere in the Thailand Jungle. They were married at Sarah's Northumberland home the following year and now have four splendid children: Alexander, Katrina, Christopher and Tristram. Meanwhile Chloe, of the rare breeds, also found a new husband at Loseley in Mike Dancey, who had worked as tractor driver on the Estate all his life.

Like Chloe, Mike was a real lover of animals and has horses of his own and he looks after his tractor with almost as much affection.

In 1992 we started charging the public £1.50 for entering the grounds. For over forty years entry to the grounds had been free. People could walk with their children and dogs round the gardens, picnic, use the play area and other facilities, and then go home without any payment. Fine, but it costs a large sum each year to keep the lawns mown, the edges trimmed, the flower borders kept up, the litter collected, the lavatories cleaned, the drive repaired. Our charge is in line with most other properties and nearly all the visitors consider it reasonable, although, as usual, there were a few who were outraged.

Several visitors have had previous connections with Loseley, including recently the son and daughter of Ward, Loseley chauffeur in the 1920s, the daughter herself having been dairymaid at Loseley before the war. Housemaids who have visited speak well of their time at Loseley, although it cannot have been an easy life. In the first year we opened, two of the visitors told the guide that they had been maids at Loseley in 1912, when the House was let to a wealthy American, Miss Dodge. Their employment ended suddenly and dramatically: there had been a spiritualist seance in the night and something terrifying had happened. Miss Dodge and all the staff moved out in the early hours of the morning and never returned. They were sworn to secrecy, so could not disclose any details. This coincides with the account which my mother gave me of the incident. She took the opportunity to warn me against becoming involved in spiritualism. Spiritualism is also among the problems we encounter in the Christian healing ministry and people should be made aware of the dangers.

Another visitor with a happier outcome is Mrs Babs Griffiths. A gentle person, slight of build and widowed many years ago, Babs was a frequent visitor to Loseley in the days of 'teas through the Scullery window'. She loved the peace of Loseley and she was a devout Christian. When we needed a volunteer to talk to the visitors about the Christian pictures, Donny, then running the Shop, at once suggested Babs and she proved ideal for that role.

People say: 'It must be awful having all these people tramping round your House, swarming over the grounds, invading your privacy.' Not at all. It is lovely to see people enjoying themselves, sharing in the beauty of Loseley, strolling along the moat border, enjoying the flowers and the water lilies, spotting the odd carp in the water, and young families with children playing on the lawn. As for the visitors to the House, we are grateful to them – for more than forty years they have played an important part in the building's survival. Most of our visitors sense the friendly, peaceful, lived-in atmosphere of the House and they themselves make their own contribution to that atmosphere. Of course, a tiny minority are dishonest, difficult or litter-bugs. The biggest irritant is the many cars that come up on days or at times, including the night, when we are not open, as is clearly marked on the signs.

Mike took over the Leisure Department in 1990. His first move was to franchise the catering, which was wise. Mike is having considerable success in building up the corporate business functions. We seem to have a special affinity with the motor industry – Rover took over all our facilities for the whole of April 1993 for the Southern Area Launch of the successful 600 model and we have had Rolls Royce, Land Rover and Ford as well as car shows and local promotions for Mercedes and Saab; and we have bookings for BMW, VW and Toyota. There is seldom a Saturday from April to October without a wedding reception in the Barn and there is an increasing number of parties and celebrations.

'Corporate Fun Days' are becoming increasingly popular: companies getting their staff down to the country for a variety of activities and tests ranging from treasure hunts to archery, go-karting and clay pigeon shooting. Loseley Opera in the garden is getting established and there have been several open-air plays. The Performing Arts Company have staged splendid concerts on the lawn with fireworks, watched by some 4,000 people. These outdoor events are really lovely when the weather is fine but thunderstorms are not unknown!

Our most difficult evening was not caused by the weather, which was warm and sunny. It was 14th July and we had allowed a promoter to hold a Bastille Ball 'in aid of charity' in the Front Park. On that evening, the final performance of *Romeo and Juliet* was taking place in the Walled Garden 200 yards away. There were certain 'misunderstandings' about times of intervals at the Ball, as well as noise levels. Trying to plead for lower sound amplification to a pop group in full swing and at full amplification is as frustrating and as ineffective as chasing a galloping sow with a thermometer! In fact it was much worse, for Mike and I were aware of the effect on the passions of Romeo, Juliet and Co. in the garden. The theatre people were so nice about it. The 'Charity' Ball organisers went into liquidation, leaving their bills unpaid except for the awful pop group who had demanded payment in advance.

Charity events have included balls, concerts and fund-raising dinners as well as outdoor activities such as the Classic Car Show. One of the most moving events has been the Marsden Hospital Forget-Me-Not Club Remembrance Days. Some 300 parents and families of children who have died of cancer come for the day. They have the use of all the facilities of the House, Garden, farm tours and Tithe Barn, and conclude with a very moving service held in the Marquee. On the last occasion, it was only at the end of the day that I discovered that the chaplain who had conducted the service was terminally ill with cancer.

Because the Barn is increasingly in use for wedding and corporate functions, Mike is having building conversions carried out in the outbuildings of the House Courtyard so that the public teas and the Shop will return to their original locations but with much better facilities than in the days of 'teas through the Scullery window'.

Mike and Sarah are creating new formal gardens in the old walled garden which will become an important feature for visitors and a change from our organic vegetables and those weeds. Loseley is accustomed to the changes as generations come and go.

In October 1995, after forty-six seasons, Sue and I hand over the running of the House to Mike and Sarah. When Sue and I first opened the House in 1950 we little thought that one day it would become part of a 'Loseley Leisure Department'. Sue laughs at the title: 'I love it – Loseley LEISURE – nothing but hard work here!' But we have enjoyed almost every moment of it.

Until recently Loseley Leisure was one department that never used professional advisers or consultants. Guildway made up for this, as we shall see.

CHAPTER 13

THE PROFESSIONALS

I started my own business within a few months of demob, with no training apart from three weeks' army resettlement courses, one on commerce and one on agriculture. I have always been aware of my lack of professionalism and expertise; I was not afraid to ask or to admit my ignorance. I believe my advisers found that a refreshing change, but I was a worry to some because, as my first financial adviser told me, I always tried to run before I could walk and certainly I was always near the overdraft limit, usually needing more.

I have emphasised my philosophy of teamwork, friendship and the importance of people. This applied also to my professional advisers, as described in the October 1963 issue of *Director* magazine, reproduced abbreviated, with permission, below.

A Mixed Manned Force for the Board

Major More-Molyneux owns a stately home near Guildford, a 500-acre farm, and most of the share capital of a private manufacturing company. At first sight he hardly fits the part of a pioneer; his occupations like his background seem orthodox by any standard. In fact, however, the home – Loseley House – is thrown open to the public at half a crown a head; the farm is run as a co-partnership; and the company is a vigorous and growing enterprise with new ideas in the unorthodox field of manufactured houses.

Last month I was asked to join in one of the company's unusual activities, a session, in the Lincoln Room at Brown's Hotel, of the Advisory Committee. Since 1959 the sales turnover of Cedar Homes has been rising at a rate of 60 per cent a year. For 1965 the target leaps to over £1 million. The company has started selling British-made houses to fastidious foreigners. Behind this success one can discern several factors, but chiefly the skilful use of talent of the kind most firms command but few intelligently exploit.

The company has a board which is ultimately responsible for its affairs and a management committee responsible for day-to-day purchasing, production and sales. Like other companies it employs a firm of accountants, a solicitor, a management consultant, an advertising and public relations organisation and an architect. Most firms are content to draw on the wisdom or the services of their experts as and when the need arises. Cedar Homes taps the knowledge and intelligence of the people already professionally associated with it by regular consultations, throwing before the Advisory Committee the problems which management and the board are facing, and inviting their comments.

The first purpose of the committee is to generate ideas and subject company projects to wide-ranging criticism. The second is to let the experts whose services the company employs know how it is developing even in fields with which they have no immediate concern.

Minutes are taken and circulated, but the sessions are fairly informal. The company's full-time executives are fully informed about the discussions that have taken place. Responsibility remains with them and the board.

The regular members of the Advisory Committee are the chairman of the company (chairing the sessions himself and taking the minutes); the company's solicitor, who is also a director, Meryn Lewis; its management consultants, Harold Norcross and Glye Hodson; its accountants, J. A. Owers and H. L. Goodman; and its advertising agents, James White and C. G. Corbett. The architect, John Brownrigg, is an occasional member.

The session I attended started at eleven o'clock, adjourned briefly for lunch, and carried on until the late afternoon. The main subject on the agenda, for example, was the manner in which Cedar Homes should develop its sales organisation in West Germany. Earlier this year, a house in sections was shipped on a lorry from Guildford to the Fertighaus 63 exhibition at Hamburg where it attracted several orders. Cedar

Homes' prices have proved to be competitive and the Germans are showing a growing interest in pre-fabricated housing. The committee was asked to help decide whether the German organisation should be a subsidiary or a branch. Here, the accountants and the solicitor sketched out the fundamentals. Meryn Lewis, who has had considerable experience abroad, argued that the all-important consideration was the impression that would be made on the German public. Merely to establish a branch office, he added, would give the impression that 'we weren't all that serious'. On the other hand, the accountants suggested, if a subsidiary were established straight away, its losses would not be available for tax relief for the parent. The chairman intervened to point out that it was not anticipated that a loss would be made after the first year. After it had been agreed that the German organisation should be a subsidiary, discussion turned to the question of what equity should be made available to the German partners.

During its session every member of the committee had something to say about subjects not usually within its competence. To the outside observer, the views of the experts in one particular field were modified by the opinions of the others with surprising frequency. Problems which at first sight looked as if they were strictly within the province of, say, the accountants or the solicitor – whether to take over another company by buying its shares or its assets, how to frame an exclusive dealer franchise – provoked useful comment from the advertising agents and the management consultant. At the end of this particular session, the chairman took away with him several firm decisions to go ahead with particular schemes or to modify them drastically. For him, the conference quite clearly brought into focus an extremely wide range of short- and long-term problems. The others present were left with a detailed and up-to-date impression of the company's current projects and problems in all their ramifications. By tea-time, when I left, the Cedar Homes Advisory Committee was peering into the future, debating the likely development of the business in the 1970s.

Very few members charged for attendance at these meetings: that was within the spirit of our relationship. Every other year or so we had an Advisory Committee dinner, with wives, and the final happy evening was at the Savoy.

Meryn Lewis, our most conscientious lawyer, was the most involved in my various activities. He was a wonderful friend and his love of nature has been mentioned earlier. Meryn loved Loseley and was every bit as dedicated as Sue and I to its survival. In his office in St James's Place, Meryn was apt to be tense; he was so efficient, abhorred sloppy work and carelessly written letters – all details had to be 100 per cent correct. On his weekend visits to Loseley Meryn always liked to look round the Estate and if we were selling a strip of land, or if there was a boundary dispute, he would want to go and see 'the body', to ensure that everything was correctly shown on the plan.

Meryn was a non-executive director of Guildway for many years and I learned much from him. He worked all hours and on one occasion telephoned me at 11 on a Sunday night to emphasise his concern about a detail in a Guildway legal contract. It was a sad day when Meryn died suddenly, just before he was due for retirement. I have come across a typical letter from him, written from his home in London on Saturday, 22nd June 1957.

This is first to thank you and Sue for a most interesting and enjoyable day on Wednesday. Secondly, to congratulate you. It was heartening to see Guildcrete in full blast and on top of most things.

I began by believing in Guildcrete and its future (houses especially included!) subject only to your being able to get the figure-work under control in time. Then came a time when I began to wonder whether my imagination had run away with my judgment.

Now, although you are still in the wood and in spite of continuing doubts about the houses, I think everybody must be convinced that Guildcrete can succeed, thanks entirely to your own courage and pertinacity. Jolly well done!

And now for streamlining the Farm and your own thermal units.

Written just over a year after the Guildcrete 'non-liquidation' meeting, this letter evidences Meryn's deep interest and concern.

As he would have wished, his widow, Gwen, came to live on Loseley Estate for her last few years.

Back in 1947, John Brownrigg, ARIBA, had done his first assignment for Guildcrete, designing a concrete eaves gutter. John always remained interested and supportive of my business ventures and was involved with Guildway housing designs from the first historic America Line brick-skin bungalow in 1960.

'Hew to the line and let the chips fall where they may' seemed a good slogan for management consultants George S. May. Guildway must have come into contact through a direct mail shot; certainly not through recommendation, and we soon terminated the assignment.

Our next consultant, Glye Hodson, was different and continued with us for over thirty years. Glye carried out a wide range of assignments for Guildway with his managers, including bonus schemes, factory layouts, organisation, MBO and sales incentives. Glye and I got on well and we discussed matters freely and openly. He later became a non-executive director of Guildway and also of Loseley Dairy Products Ltd, where he had also done consultancy work. After my retirement Glye continued to help Mike as a member of the Farming Partnership Committee and, now in retirement, remains one of Loseley's 'elder statesmen' and he and Marjorie and family will always remain friends.

Accountancy has never been my strong point so good accountants were essential. I was fortunate in having the brilliant Gillie Potier at the time of our greatest financial crisis and the 'non-liquidation' saga. John Owers took over from Gillie. Tall, slim, dark-haired with a neat moustache, John was bright and very calm: he had been a Spitfire photographic pilot in the war, flying at high altitude without any armament. It would have suited his temperament and he claims to have thoroughly enjoyed it. John took a deep interest in the business and however horrendous the situation, John would say 'I don't think you need worry. Come and have lunch at the Club and we'll sort it out.' John would never think of charging for those meetings that he hosted over lunch and he could always be relied on to produce a helpful solution.

John wrote a history of Limebeer and Company which included the following extract: '. . . when Gilbert Potier decided to join Consolidated Goldfields in 1957 he asked me to take over this client and took me down to Guildford to introduce me. It was apparent that great progress had been made on the rehabilitation of the Farm and Estate but the company was not particularly profitable and was giving cause for concern. JRMM was working tirelessly on both the Estate and the business. I spent many hours at long meetings there over the next few years. There were some very successful years and spectacular growth in exports. The Queen's Award to Industry was won in 1972. Harry Goodman made a major contribution and, soon after he became a partner in 1963, he took over control of this client's affairs, although I remain an Adviser to JRMM and am a member of his Advisory Committee. As often happens, through our professional activities we have become personal friends.' Very sadly, John died within a month of retiring. I had the privilege of reading the Lesson at his Memorial Service in St Clement Danes Church, in which Anne Donne is buried.

On Guildway business, Harry Goodman came with me on two visits to the Guildway (Deutschland) office in Hamburg and also on a rather wild assignment in the west of Ireland where we had considered buying a joinery company. When we got there it was clear that I did not need an accountant to tell me that it was dodgy and no deal was done. The Irish MD had excused himself in the middle of our talks to play a round of golf! Harry was also a Methodist preacher so we were able to talk of other things besides business on our trips. He became a Trustee of the Loseley Christian Trust and at the age of 50 courageously gave up his profession to become a full-time ordained Minister on the Gower Peninsula, supported by his wife Mavis, also an active Christian.

Our advertising budget was always small and I continued to direct the advertising myself until after Fred had retired as MD. Advertising agents are necessary and to a large extent you get what you pay for: one needs good creative people with imagination. Solicitor, accountant, architect and industrial consultant: we stayed loyal to them for thirty years or until they retired or died. Advertising agents we changed quite often, though we never actually fell out with any of them: the very good ones either got too expensive or, understandably, put less good people on to our relatively small account. We made little use of PR consultants but had two unfortunate experiences. One PR consultant had total disregard for the truth. Discussing publicising the delivery of Guildway's 1,000th house, he suggested in all seriousness 'Why not say it's the 10,000th? It sounds much more impressive.' That was the end of him. Some years later we were truthfully able to announce a production rate of one house per hour; that *was* impressive but we did not employ a PR consultant to tell the Press.

A London-based PR consultancy offered to prepare some PR proposals for us. If we liked what they had produced, the firm would put their proposals into action and charge their normal fee. With the assurance that we could not lose, we wrote accepting the offer. A few weeks later the proposals arrived. Some were too complex, others too expensive and the remainder childish. We wrote and politely declined. To our surprise we then received an account for the preparation of the proposals. We replied, pointing out the agreed terms, under which no payment whatever was due. Next we received a final warning. When in London, I took the trouble to call on the Chairman to point out the facts. I wasted my time. A writ followed, and I appeared before the Judge in a London court.

'Did you make use of the proposals that were prepared for you?'
'No, your Honour.'
'Why did you not use them?'
'Because we thought they were a load of rubbish.'
'And some would agree with you,' said the Judge and we won the case. Not very good PR for the PR company!

A number of friends who were in business were occasional members of the Advisory Committee, including my old schoolfriend, Mike Bradstock, Chairman of University Motors, founded by his father, and other businesses. Mike always took an interest in Guildway; he was more successful than myself at making money, but not as successful as his young brother David, who founded the insurance firm Bradstocks.

Sir Claud, mentioned earlier with the ghost and the clock, also attended the Advisory on occasion when he was down from Scotland. Claud is a one-off, a man with a very independent mind. He would never be rushed, was usually right and always ready for a laugh. Claud did some excellent engineering work at Guildway, designing and installing pneumatic cramps on the benches and other devices. His advice on management matters was sound, though not always orthodox. Claud created a stir at an Advisory Meeting: asked if he would like one lump of sugar or two in this coffee, he replied 'Six please!' Asked how many children he has, Claud, the engineer, replies 'One of each and

100 per cent spares'; to ordinary mortals this is four and I am proud to have one as a god-daughter.

Business is different in the 1990s from the 1960s: with increasing emphasis on money, clients have become 'profit centres' – my Advisory Committee members would have been horrified. Partners and managers of large professional firms are under great pressure to increase fee income from each client: if they fail to do so there may well be redundancies. I have seen this happen. Excessive charges to Loseley by two separate professional firms have been blamed on the computer. These charges were rectified, but computers need watching: they are apt to charge you for hosting their bosses to lunch!

Loseley's present advisers are efficient and we are grateful to them and regard them as personal friends. Mike is also fortunate in having on his Partners' Committee Alistair Walker, retired Harrods Director and Food Hall Manager, as well as an agricultural adviser and an accountant.

I was really upset when, many years ago, a farm foreman referred to my secretary as 'the girl in the office'. Secretaries to me are very important people, easing one's passage through each day; the more hectic the pace the more important becomes the secretary/PA. Good secretaries are true professionals, completely unselfish, putting your interest before their own and at times even before their family's. Loyalty and dedication, sometimes to a degree that is embarrassing. I have been very fortunate: I realise that not all secretaries are like this!

A secretary needs to know your mind and who you would wish to see, who are the time-wasters to be turned away. She will never make excuses to you but will be prepared to make excuses for you, lending a constructive ear to your problems, never intruding by mentioning hers. I never thought of my secretary as an employee but as a colleague and friend; we have shared many laughs and only twice can I remember tears.

The farm secretary I inherited in 1946 was an admirable little lady, although not within my specification. Bordering on retirement, Miss Bolton was kind and respectable, her dark hair had turned mainly to grey; soft-spoken and polite, she wore steel-rimmed spectacles. Miss B. came in from 11am till 4pm, typed slowly with two fingers and did not take shorthand. Slightly prim, Miss Bolton will always be remembered by the word 'effers'. It appeared in a report that she typed for the herdsman: the dictionary spells it 'heifers'.

Apart from that, Miss Bolton did something for Loseley that no highly-trained efficient secretary could ever have achieved. With two words, Miss B. made thousands of pounds for Loseley. The two words were 'Esq.' and 'Private'. We proposed selling Binscombe Farm, outlying on the south of the Estate, rented by F. R. Stovold Ltd, and sub-let to Mr Podger. Before 29th September I dictated to Miss B. a letter terminating the tenancy on that date. Because of a new Act of Parliament, if we failed to give notice by that date the tenancy would be protected. Miss B. addressed the envelope to F. R. Stovold Esq., not to the company, and marked the envelope 'Private'. Unfortunately FRS Esq. was abroad and the 'Private' envelope remained unopened. When FRS received it on his return the notice was out of time and invalid. Miss B. was more upset than I was when she realised what she had done and had to be consoled, not castigated. Unfortunately the next year, under the 1947 Act, Godalming Town Council compulsorily purchased 40 acres of Binscombe Farm for housing at £100 per acre. Later more land went for building and we got over £1,000 per acre and other small parcels followed. In the end we received as much from the sales of building land than we should have obtained for the whole farm including land, house and buildings if we had sold in Miss B.'s time. Soon afterwards Miss B. retired and was allocated a home at the splendid Whitely Village, of which our friend and previous agent Colin Bardwell is now Chairman.

Our next secretary was Miss Bennett, middle-aged and blonde who got on well with everyone. Although more than two-fingered, she was not quick and with life at Loseley getting more and more busy she left after two years or so. Miss Bennett has her place in Loseley history for repeating to me the remark by one of the farm chaps that I was a mean old so-and-so, which led to the formation of the Loseley Co-Partnership, and she is included in the photograph of the first JPC Meeting.

Miss Clarke, known as 'Clarkie', was the next secretary. In her late 30s, strong with a rather deep voice, ex-WRAC Senior NCO, very competent, loyal and hard-working. Clarkie was enthusiastic and prepared to help out with any job that needed doing. She seemed as sad as we all were when she left: having received an inheritance Clarkie decided to take up some project in Pembrokeshire; it sounded dicey to us and sadly it did not turn out well. Sue and I visited her a few years later, by then working at a garage at Haverfordwest and she died not long afterwards.

Next as secretary was Barbara, a very active 17-year-old, who cycled daily to Loseley in all weathers from Jacobs Well, seven miles away. Barbara was bright, keen, quick and efficient and got on well with everyone. She was a keen Christian and helped to start a Sunday School in Littleton. Two years or so after Barbara joined us I appointed our first farm manager. Richard was eligible, a nice guy, fair and good-looking. Barbara was fond of him and he was not running away. Then we took on Beryl as book-keeper. Not slim and lively as Barbara, more the maternal type. Beryl also became aware of Richard and she had two advantages over Barbara; she did not have to cycle home every evening, residing in the Stable Flat at Loseley, and she was an excellent cook. Sadly for Barbara, it was Beryl that got him. Shortly afterwards Barbara left to train as a nursing missionary, then married a fellow student and went out to Africa. Tragically, Barbara's husband was killed in a car accident. Barbara returned to England and is now a grandmother, living with her second husband, Graham, in a Guildway bungalow at Jacobs Well, deeply involved with their church.

Daphne Holloway came as farm secretary/book-keeper and we all know what happened to her: 'Shall I make a cheese?'

Marion, who had started with us as head of the Guildway typing pool, became Mike's secretary. Marion was middle-aged, small, bright and cheerful, loyal and efficient. Sadly, Marion's husband died just before she retired. She lives locally and one of her sons, Howard and his wife are missionaries.

From the time that Daphne joined, my secretaries were employed by Guildway. They had a very wide variety of work, from Guildway matters, farming, Estate, charities, minutes, voluntary service, later Surrey Lieutenancy and Shrievalty and, increasingly, Christian papers on the healing ministry, sermons, Christian Heritage and mystical pictures. I usually put these on tape. On one occasion I told my secretary Clare that there was a Christian piece on the tape. 'It really is a bit deep,' I warned, 'I had my eyes shut as I dictated it.' 'Don't worry,' Clare gaily responded, 'I'll type it with my eyes shut.' After that, all my recorded Christian thoughts were known as 'eyes shut' pieces.

Sylvia Hazlitt joined Guildway as my secretary soon after her marriage in 1959. She was lovely and very efficient. She became the first editor of *Guildway News* and continued for most of the publication's thirty-three years, although the birth of her first child Mark necessitated handing over as my secretary to Deirdre. Sadly, Sylvia's husband Nigel died suddenly in his 40s and years later she re-married. She is still associated with Loseley, managing the Farm Shop and organising our annual Christmas Fair in the Barn.

Deirdre, from Australia, was fun. She had really auburn hair, and was previously secretary to the Director of Sydney Opera House. Deirdre was cultured, with a rugger-playing husband, Keith, that she had tried to 'civilise', taking him to Shakespeare plays and opera, both of which unfortunately sent him to sleep. Deirdre apologised for 'not being very churchified' but, like all my secretaries, she coped excellently without complaint. After five years Deirdre and Keith returned to Australia but we keep in touch and they have twice been back with their daughters. Rita followed, a great naturalist, keen writer and publicity girl. She was long-legged with dark flashing eyes, a good figure and did not lack male attention. Rita was also an efficient secretary but I lost her to the publicity department and later had the pleasure of proposing her health at her wedding.

Margaret was one of the few that was not a success, soon deciding that being my secretary for both Guildway and Loseley was too much. She demanded an assistant. I declined and she left. Fred, then Managing Director of Guildway, generously offered an immediate replacement by sharing his secretary, Christine West. Christine, in her mid-20s and recently married to John, an insurance broker, had joined as Fred's secretary a few months earlier. The Managing Director's secretary has a full-time job but Christine is special. Small, dark-haired and Austrian by birth, Christine is full of energy and puts everything into her work. She coped splendidly not only with the Guildway work for both Fred and myself, but the Loseley business as well, working at Loseley in the morning and at Guildway in the afternoon, and she did not ask for an assistant. What a girl! Christine never complained to me that Fred had given her too much work nor to Fred about the load I had put on her.

Christine, like Deirdre and others, was 'not very churchified', and she arrived as my secretary at a very active Christian period, with Eve, Berthe Hess and her picture and Christian Heritage Year (see chapter 15). At times I know that she felt I was 'going over the top' with mysticism, yet she never complained. Christine was always working, never chatting or wasting time: with Fred and I to cope with there wasn't any time to waste. Christine and John bought a plot of land on the Loseley Estate and had a Guildway house built. Soon afterwards their first son, James, was born. I had been resigned to the fact that I would never find anyone to match Christine but, worse than that, her replacement and I just did not begin to get on. I told Christine of the problem and she at once said that if I was prepared to come to her house, situated between Loseley and Guildway, she would be happy to take up again as my secretary. We had a Guildway phone line put into her home, and looking after a baby and me was no greater problem than looking after Fred and me: Fred will not take this amiss! When Christine's second son Timmy was born, it was time for me to move on, but it was to be 'au revoir' and not goodbye.

'Eyes shut' Clare arrived. Clare was young, tall and fair, a happy, sociable girl and a great animal-lover. After Clare's first year I moved my office from Guildway to the Loseley Billiard Room and she must have missed the companionship of all the people at Guildway. After seven years Clare moved on, but we still keep in touch. Clare Slemeck had often mentioned her uncle, killed in a daring wartime operation. Years later I discovered that the uncle so revered, yet of course never seen by Clare, had been my schoolfriend, David Napier, who had stroked the winning House IV, which I coxed, and we were both in the Eight at Henley.

Nicola came through an agency. They could not speak highly enough of this wonderful girl, so dedicated, so efficient, so hard-working. I am suspicious of agencies but this time, if anything, they underestimated Nicola. She is pure gold, utterly unselfish and never complains. I have yet to see Nicola not working for an instant. When I retired as Chairman she became Mike's secretary but is 'doing a Christine' and Mike and I are both so grateful to her. At closing time, after a busy day Nicola will ask plaintively 'Isn't there anything else you would like me to do?' As well as all the business and personal work, for Mike and me, including our various committees, Nicola took over the accounts as well as the correspondence for both the Charitable Trusts, as secretary/treasurer and applies for church covenant tax rebates, among many tasks voluntarily undertaken.

Yes, I have been lucky in my professional advisers and in my secretaries. I would not have got far without them and I am most grateful to them all.

With so many people giving their services to help me I found it difficult to turn down requests to help others by serving in voluntary work.

CHAPTER 14

VOLUNTARY PUBLIC SERVICE

I was so hectic with Loseley and Guildcrete that I had every excuse for avoiding voluntary work. I have never had ambitions in public life and, shy by nature, I am not a good committee person. Yet public service is rightly expected from the owner of Loseley, in the tradition of my ancestors, going back to the great Sir William More. I never volunteered but gradually found myself getting involved in a wide variety of unpaid commitments. Things got rather too hectic, including one evening when I had three separate meetings, leaving the first before it ended and arriving late at the next. I decided never to do that again.

In the early years almost all my voluntary work was in the evenings: I could not have been away during working hours. Sue was my great enabler – 'I'll do that for you,' she would say. She did all the chores, ensured that we never ran out of household supplies and did all the fiddly DIY jobs that husbands usually do – mending fuses, changing bulbs and plugs, coaxing stiff locks and errant clocks with WD40; and 101 other jobs, as well as keeping the rooms in show condition. Nowadays we have a large oil-fired central heating boiler and when it fails to come on Sue knows just where and how hard to kick it. Being so tied up with work, I must have been a bad parent and Sue more than made up for the lack of time that I was able to spend with our son; little wonder that he never wanted to get involved in the Guildway business.

By taking on voluntary work we were not worried about missing out on social life. We had seldom gone out socially or to the cinema (this was pre-TV!); and Sue says, 'We were too tired anyway by evening: I remember going to sleep over supper.' By day we were far too busy to hunt, shoot, fish, play golf or go racing; in any case, these activities would have seemed dull compared to working to meet the challenge.

In the second year after my post-war return to Loseley I found myself elected Churchwarden at St Nicholas, Compton, a position I was to hold for twenty years. My father had been Churchwarden before the war and great-great-uncle George was Rector at Compton for forty-nine years. I am now on the Parochial Church Council and a Lay Pastoral Assistant.

I was for a time on the National Council for Guide Dogs for the Blind, having been Founder President of the Guildford Branch, and I was also Founder Chairman of Guildford and District Productivity Council. Later, experience of a different kind was as a member of the Management Committee of the Hydon Hill Cheshire Home: the residential accommodation had been supplied by my company Guildway. Running a Cheshire Home to very high standards calls for great dedication from the management, care staff and volunteers. The award of the MBE to Mrs Joan Inskipp for her dedicated work for Hydon Hill and disabled people was joyously celebrated by a Hydon Hill Tea Party.

I am the third successive generation of the family to serve as Trustee of the Guildford Poyle Charity. I was for several years on the Surrey Rural Industries Committee and COSIRA, and for some twenty-five years have been a Vice President of Surrey Voluntary Services Council. I have been a President or Patron of a number of local organisations and appeals including the Surrey Association of Youth Clubs and PHAB (Physically Handicapped Able Bodied), and of the Friends of the Brookwood and Milford Hospitals, and associated with many other causes. I have been on endless fund-raising committees for a wide variety of charities. Like most people, fund-raising is not my favourite activity, particularly as it involves 'putting in a word', i.e. begging, to the same generous friends.

An unusual fund-raising committee was that of St Marylebone Church, London, which included funding the work of converting the vaults into a Christian Healing Centre.

From its inception I served on the Council of the Phyllis Tuckwell Hospice under the Chairmanship of the founder, surgeon Sir Edward Tuckwell, whose wife Phyllis had died of cancer. The great Sir George Edwards OM, CBE, FRS, Chairman of the Executive Committee, had himself suffered from cancer. 'Eddie did some gardening in my lower regions,' was his typical comment. Situated in Farnham, in a small converted National Health Service Hospital, the Hospice is low-key and not architecturally impressive but it has a lovely atmosphere and a wonderful caring team. It also has a chapel. Caring is the most vital ingredient of all hospices, and the staff-to-patient ratio is the big difference between a hospice and a hospital.

I never volunteered, but found it difficult to turn down good causes. As for Chairmanship of the Surrey University Local Industry Committee, not only did I not volunteer but I wasn't even asked. The first I knew of the appointment was on attending a meeting in London and seeing my name projected on the screen as Chairman! My appeal to the Chancellor, Lord Robens, that I was too heavily committed was met with a typically charming assurance that the job would not be onerous or time-consuming, but this unfortunately proved over-optimistic. It did, however, bring me into contact with several progressive industrialists, including my Chairman for the Guildford area, John Smith, Managing Director of Dennis, until he was imprisoned for seven years in Iraq by Saddam Hussein, surviving on the Bible, Marmite, and the loyal support of family and friends.

Voluntary public service of a different kind was membership of the Martin Working Party, set up by the Rank Foundation to decide what practices in modern agriculture were unacceptable from the Christian standpoint. This was a very interesting assignment with technical experts, environmentalists, animal husbandry professors and a Canon (now Bishop of Dorchester) among others. We were concerned at several aspects of factory farming and animals kept intensively under unnatural conditions. We learned that pigs kept intensively indoors were susceptible to new viruses which built up faster than vaccines could be developed. Unnatural intensive conditions demand a very high standard of management. I personally put a very high priority on our stewardship of the livestock in our keeping. As I stated to the Working Party, I believe that an animal should have the opportunity of enjoying itself – such as a lamb jumping for joy, a hen scratching in the litter. In our Loseley Farm leaflet I included:

We acknowledge our responsibility for the welfare of our animals and aim to keep them contented and healthy. We will not permit unnecessary discomfort or suffering to stock in any circumstances. Although often more profitable, *we are opposed to the live shipment of animals for slaughter abroad.*

We will never be involved in battery hens, intensive veal or any similar unnatural processes.

We prefer natural methods where possible. No chemicals or inorganic fertilisers are used in the market garden or on organic cereals. No artificial colouring, flavouring or preservatives are used in the dairy products or bakery products.

Some of the offices held by Sir William More, including that of Ulnager of the Cloth (Quality Controller), were salaried. I had just one salaried position. For nine years I served as a part-time Director of Seeboard, having been appointed during the Labour Government, serving when Anthony Benn was Secretary of State for Energy, continuing during Mrs Thatcher's time under Nigel Lawson, David Howell and Peter Walker. The Board met monthly at Head Office at Hove and Area Offices in Surrey, Sussex and Kent. I have happy memories of my time with Seeboard and a high regard for my colleagues and senior officers. Seeboard gave good service and labour relations were also good with increasing job flexibility. At the end of my service, Sue and I were entertained to a farewell dinner at Headquarters and typically, George Squair, Chairman at that time, called in the kitchen staff at the end of the meal and thanked them. As well as the lovely decanter from my colleagues, I was also presented with an illuminated testimonial, more than generous in its assessment of my small contribution to Seeboard, the only 'reference' I have received in my life.

In 1974 I was appointed High Sheriff of Surrey for the year, the sixth member of the family to hold this office, now over 1,000 years old. Two years earlier I had a visit from a distinguished past High Sheriff, Philip Henman. He came on what was evidently a very busy day, for our talk was interrupted by telephone messages, callers, lorry drivers wanting to know where to tip their loads. Philip, a very kind, conscientious and successful man, said just before leaving: 'You really will have to delegate all this before you become High Sheriff.' I didn't delegate, but somehow I coped. Fortunately the duties of the High Sheriff today are not as burdensome as in Elizabethan times. Nowadays ceremonial duties include attending on the Judges daily for two weeks in the Crown Court, and attending official openings, special services, mayoral receptions and banquets. There is opportunity for taking personal initiatives and supporting special causes in the county.

In many of my speeches I called for public support for the Police in their difficult task. I also emphasised the importance of true values and the virtues which made Britain great but are now regarded as 'square', including courage, loyalty and truth. I had the privilege of opening the new Guildford Divisional Police Station and the plaque with my name remains above the main desk, which proved helpful on one occasion when collecting someone from the cells! The Guildford pub bombings also took place during my Year of Office and I toured the scene with the Home Secretary, Roy Jenkins, together with the Chief Constable and the Mayor. During my year as High Sheriff I was the guest at Grand Day Dinner of Mr Justice Goff when he was Treasurer of Lincoln's Inn, the position once held by our family connection, Sir Thomas More.

In the Crown Court weeks, the Sheriff attends on the Judge and gives lunches each day and attends church services at the beginning of each of the two weeks. We also gave dinners for the Judges and for the Surrey Constabulary at Loseley.

The Revd Dick Hambly, then Rector for Compton, was my Chaplain and he attended many of the official occasions. Dick was with Sue and I when we visited Coldingly Prison, where we lunched with the Governor and his wife; I put in my notes: 'A prison to be proud of!' We also visited the Guildford Probation Office and had long discussions on the problems and ways in which the community and industry could help. Much more could be done in this direction.

I attended the Presentation of New Colours to my father's Regiment, the Queens, by Queen Margarita of Denmark. The Colonel at the time was our relation Major General Fergus Ling CBE CB DSO MC. My Shrievalty Year had coincided with the creation of the new local authorities, which came into existence on 1st April 1974.

A very rewarding part of our Year was meeting people who were doing caring work among the disadvantaged, the sick, the young and the offenders. It was heartening to discover the vast number of people in unpaid voluntary work over a very wide field.

Many individuals deserve a mention, but one who must not be omitted is Lady Heald CBE (Daphne), now in her nineties. All her adult life she has been involved in voluntary work, mainly in the field of Red Cross, St John and Nursing Charities. Indefatigable, she is still involved with many charities, usually as active President or Chairman. She travels by train to London for meetings, doing her correspondence on the journey, and on returning in the evening often hosts in her home a charity function. She also opens her lovely gardens in aid of the Nursing Charity.

In 1976 I was appointed a DL (Deputy Lieutenant) of Surrey, an appointment also held by my great-grandfather James, and in 1983 I was appointed Vice Lord Lieutenant to Lord Hamilton, then Lord Lieutenant. There are some fifty DLs in the county but only one Vice Lord Lieutenant, so my position is equivalent to that of Sir William More's of Deputy Lord Lieutenant; but fortunately I am spared his responsiblity for raising the army in the county. I was re-appointed to the position by Lord Hamilton's successor, Mr Richard Thornton OBE JP, the first commoner to be appointed Lord Lieutenant of Surrey. The main duty of the Vice Lord Lieutenant is to represent the Lord Lieutenant in the county when he is unable to be present, particularly on Royal visits. Sue has on several occasions been in attendance with me, including twice with Her Majesty the Queen.

By 1980 I had got myself over-involved in voluntary work and something had to be done. I have before me a draft letter dated October 1980:

I do hate saying no and I have got myself over-committed. There are so many good works and organisations which one would like to help but apart from my business commitments I am involved in a large number of Christian and charitable causes. I am convinced that the Christian message is more significant today and more needed than ever; if I was starting all over again I might well have devoted myself full-time to Christian service. My colleagues have been concerned at the number of voluntary commitments I have taken on. My responsibility for those who work with us and others who depend on us dictates that I must give more attention to the businesses. There is a limit to what any individual can do effectively, therefore I regret that I am unable to take on any fresh commitments and I do hope you will understand.

Sue is Royal British Legion Area Poppy Appeal organiser and, with assistance from her sister Donny, personally calls on all the houses in her area in the evenings, ensuring that no one is missed. She is also on a number of other charity committees as well as being involved in the Loseley Charities and our Christian work. Mike also plays his part. He has served on the County Committee of the Country Landowners' Association, was Chairman of Surrey Farming and Wildlife Advisory Group and of the Guildford Branch of the Surrey Society (CPRE); he is on the Committee of the Farmers' Club, a past School Governor and the fourth successive generation of the family to serve on the Artington Parish Council. He is also a member of the Council of the Surrey County Agricultural Society.

Nowadays my time and Sue's is increasingly devoted to Christian work including daily intercessions for the sick and bereaved and visiting sick people in hospital and at home and membership of prayer groups. The Christian Cancer Help Centre is a very important part of our work, described in a later chapter. Our Centre is associated with Acorn Christian Healing Trust founded by Bishop Morris and Anne Maddocks, of which I am a founder Apostolate member. Acorn is a resource for the development of the Christian healing ministry and has had a considerable influence on the growth of this ministry within the Churches. Membership includes priests, medics and laymen. The three-day conference is a great meeting ground and highlight of the year.

I am also a member of the Lambeth Partnership which supports the Archbishop's initiatives in promoting Christian faith and awareness in this Decade of Evangelism.

I give talks to groups and societies about faith, the healing ministry and cancer support and encourage people to start new Christian initiatives, using their own homes; particularly the formation of more Christian Cancer Support Groups. When I receive an invitation to speak to clubs or associations on the subject of Loseley, I make the condition that I will include our Christian work, which I now regard as the most important of my activities. It is encouraging that this is usually well received.

There is so much more that needs doing: 'The fields are white unto harvest.' I almost forgot, on Sundays Sue and I normally attend at church!

An unexpected second experience of God was to lead me into a new field of Christian work.

CHAPTER 15

THE CALL AND THE ENABLING

On a Tuesday evening in January 1976 Fred Gooch told me his terrible news: the surgeon had just informed him that his wife, Joan, was terminally ill with cancer. Later that evening I was due to attend a prayer meeting. I had never been to a prayer meeting before so I got there a few minutes early and talked with the leader of the group, Bronwen Astor, a Roman Catholic convert. I told Bronwen about Fred's wife and Arthur, another Guildway friend, also dying of cancer.

The prayer meeting was held in a comfortable, panelled room with a log fire. About ten of us sat round in a semi-circle and the meeting commenced with a recorded talk by a Cardinal Suenens. After a pause someone asked for a certain hymn which we sang and this was followed by a deep silence, a Bible reading, a prayer. Then it happened . . . Bronwen said: 'James has two people he wants us to pray for.' Bronwen was sitting across the room from me, seven or eight paces away. What happened next was as sudden as it was fleeting in duration. It is not easy to describe – at the time, as Bronwen was speaking, it felt as though a swarm of bees was coming from Bronwen, straight through my forehead. Not real bees, of course, but energy, perhaps electricity: as Bronwen explained some days later, it was in fact the power of the Holy Spirit that I was experiencing.

Although the experience lasted but a moment, the effect was permanent. From that instant, I had enhanced compassion and felt led to visit sick people in hospital, I was able to meditate and felt the need to do so and I had an understanding of the nature of God.

I don't know how it happened, but in that fraction of a second my life was changed. How did I know that this was from God? Because it took place at a Christian prayer meeting where we were praising God, hearing His Word in Bible reading, singing His praise in hymns. There was also close similarity with that evening in June 1958 in Wales, when I was also praying and experienced the love, the presence, the glory of God. Who but God would be giving me awareness of His presence, of His nature? Anyone who has received the Holy Spirit will understand this experience. Others will have real difficulty and I sympathise with them, because up to that moment I myself would have had difficulty in understanding it. I had not asked for this, all I asked was prayer for two people suffering from cancer. It took me several weeks to realise it, but God's response had equipped me for ministry to cancer patients. I was now discovering God's purpose for me, and not before time: at the age of 16 I had felt that God would have a purpose for me, and I was now over 55: no time to waste.

Some weeks later a Guildway mechanic, 33-year-old Harry Edwards, developed Hodgkins' lymphoma, cancer-related. A good-looking man, with fair hair and blue eyes, Harry was clean featured and looked younger than his 33 years. Often with a smile on his lips, he was one of those kind and cheerful people it is always a pleasure to meet and it was a great shock to us all to know that Harry was very ill. I visited Harry at home and in hospital a number of times. His condition deteriorated further and he was moved to the intensive care ward at the County Hospital. His parents were informed that all his functions were failing: he would not survive for more than two days, it might be only a few hours. Surprisingly, I was allowed into the intensive care ward. Harry was unconscious and the nurse moved out of the ward as I entered. I laid my hands on his head, as the channel for God's healing love, and I prayed for healing. Three days later Harry was moved from intensive care into a cancer ward and when I entered he was sitting up drinking tea. He made steady progress and in six months was back at Guildway, working part-time.

I told his parents, who were not Church people: 'We must thank God for Harry's recovery.' 'Oh, of course, we have prayed and we give thanks to God,' they responded, but they did not know that I had prayed and laid hands on him. I knew that it was God's doing, but I felt inhibited from saying more for his parents would have given me the credit. Working in pairs obviates this problem. A year later Harry died and the family, his fiancée, our chaplain and myself were present during his final minutes. The extra year had given the family and Harry time to come to terms with death.

At the time of Harry's illness a mutual friend had told me about Eve, a 26-year-old hospital nurse, very ill with cancer in the Westminster Hospital. She was in a great deal of pain, she was fearful, had no faith and was often in tears; Eve's husband was an army corporal who could not accept the situation and was no help to her. I wrote to Eve saying that I was certain that she could be helped by God, although at that advanced stage she might not be physically healed. I explained that I was not an ordained minister but I had a deep faith and would be happy to visit her in hospital: I would quite understand if she did not want a visit. A few days later Eve telephoned, inviting me to visit and I went up to the Westminster Hospital on the Sunday evening.

Eve was a lovely girl with deep brown eyes and black hair, which I was soon to discover was a wig: she had lost her hair through chemotherapy. The first meeting was quite relaxed; we chatted and I talked of the Lord and His love. 'No use talking to me about eternal life: I'm not a Christian, I never go to church,' said Eve. I assured her that God loved her and mentioned that even the robber crucified with our Lord had received the assurance: 'This day you will be with me in Paradise.' I asked Eve if she would like me to pray and she readily assented. I laid my hands on her head and prayed slowly and softly.

After that I visited Eve weekly, signing the office mail before leaving at 5.30pm, going first to the lovely hospital chapel to pray and prepare. At 5pm one afternoon, sitting at my desk, I had the overwhelming feeling that I must go at once to the hospital. I arrived at about 6pm to be met by Eve's husband and twin sister. 'So sorry, James, you have made an abortive journey; no one is allowed to see Eve this evening. She is under anaesthetic and being examined to find the cause of serious internal bleeding; she is losing six pints of blood a day. We tried to telephone you to stop you coming but you had left early. We are going home now: we thought at least we should wait until you came.'

As the others left, I knew that I was going to see Eve. I went to the chapel for half an hour and prayed for Eve and for all those caring for her. I meditated, then sensed that the time had come to see her. I went to Eve's curtained cubicle in Marie Celeste Ward. One nurse was coming out and, as I entered, another was tucking up the blankets. Eve's husband and twin sister had been turned away, yet here was I, being allowed in without question. I knelt by the bedside and Eve, just coming round from the anaesthetic, whispered, barely audibly: 'I'm going to Jesus.' I softly replied: 'Not yet, Eve.'

I was overjoyed to hear those words from Eve; only a few weeks before she had said: 'No good talking to me about eternal life!' That night the operation took place to locate the internal bleeding; there was no indication of the source until, instinctively, one of the surgeons put his finger on a spot and blood spurted. The cause identified, the bleeding was cured. Eve did get better and became strong enough to come down to Loseley with her husband for a weekend, but sadly after a few months she relapsed again. Eve received the sacrament of anointing with holy oil from my friend Father James Naters SSJE and died peacefully. It was our friend Mary Potier, Gillie's widow, who had originally told me about Eve, and she came with Sue and me to the funeral in Devon.

A few months after Eve died I was on a Retreat at Westminster, led by Father James Naters who had anointed Eve. In the afternoon I walked along the Embankment and passing the Westminster Hospital I thought of Eve and of similar patients now in that hospital, fearful, in pain, without faith or awareness of God. 'What can we do?' I asked myself. I went and prayed in Westminster Cathedral. On my return to the Retreat House Father Naters said: 'There is someone you may be able to help, a Jewish artist called Berthe Hess, with a gallery near St Paul's. She has painted a picture, which she asserts was inspired by God, of "The Living Christ". The picture is quite powerful and the artist believes its purpose is to bring awareness of our Lord's love and compassion to the sick, the suffering and the dying.' 'Amazing!' I exclaimed, 'that has been on my mind all afternoon – how to bring awareness of God to those who are sick, suffering and dying.'

I went to meet Berthe Hess and her daughter Mauricette and to see the picture in the gallery. It was a strange picture, certainly powerful; it was haunting and yes, it could have been inspired by God, especially in view of the extraordinary coincidence that I heard of the picture at a time when my greatest concern was to bring awareness of God's love and compassion to the sick and the suffering – the very message of the picture. There is a deep sadness in the face, particularly the eyes. It is dramatic, in built-up oils, applied with a palette-knife, a technique developed by Berthe Hess.

When the picture was being painted, Mauricette had felt that the eyes were too sad: Berthe then painted them out and started again but the result was exactly the same sadness, confirming that sadness was God's intended theme. Christ had suffered humiliation and crucifixion in order to redeem the world and those eyes now looked upon the rejection of the Father's commandments, of Jesus' own teaching, upon the hatred, the violence, the greed, the starvation, the suffering. How could His eyes be anything but sad? Mauricette also had a very vivid dream: she was looking at a wooden image of our Lord in a church and the figure fell to the floor and broke into scores of little pieces; then the pieces suddenly came together and became a man, who rose up – a Jewish girl dreaming of the Resurrection.

Berthe wished to have 'The Living Christ' unveiled in St Paul's Cathedral and asked me to arrange this. First I approached the Reverend Dr Martin Israel, a leading mystic and author, lecturer at the Royal College of Surgeons, and we lunched together with Berthe and Mauricette and viewed the picture. Berthe, in her 50s, dark and heavily built, French by birth; some would have labelled her 'Bohemian'. Mauricette, in her late 20s, already a ballet teacher, devoted to her mother and to the cause of the picture. An attractive, lively girl, sensitive but with a smile never far away.

Martin considered the picture to be inspired by God. Armed with Martin's verdict, I knocked on the door of Dean Webster of St Paul's without an appointment. It was the first time we had met, but he walked with me to the gallery. He was not too happy about the picture until I mentioned Martin Israel's commendation; this immediately demolished all misgivings and the picture was unveiled in the crypt of St Paul's by the Dean, assisted by the Reverend Dr Martin Israel, in May 1984.

A few weeks after the unveiling I became aware that 1984 was designated 'Christian Heritage Year', commemorating all who, down the centuries, had assisted in making known the Christian message and spreading the Gospel. This encompassed the Saints, martyrs, missionaries and mystics, translators and printers of the Bible, architects and builders of cathedrals, painters of sacred pictures, composers of music, writers of hymns, the authors. It seemed an opportunity to collect together the Christian pictures in the House and hang them on the Main Staircase to form a Pilgrimage for the thousands of visitors to the House. In our leaflet for Christian Heritage Year at Loseley I mentioned our connections through Waverley Abbey, St Thomas More and Dr John Donne. After detailing the Staircase Pilgrimage I ended: 'The need for spiritual awareness in today's materialist world is very great and that need can be met . . . Miracles are happening today and the Christian healing ministry is being rekindled throughout the world.'

The pictures commence with a 1516 Flemish Triptych of the Nativity, then the Baptism of Jesus by John in the River Jordan. Our Lord's Teaching Ministry is represented by a picture of the Samaritan Woman at the Well, a relaxed Jesus telling her about 'The Waters of Life'. On the opposite wall hangs a specially commissioned picture by Helen Perrott depicting some of our Lord's Healing Miracles. We then ascend the Staircase to the middle landing for a set of three large pictures – the Agony in the Garden, the Crucifixion and the Entombment. Next, the Resurrection, represented by a picture of Mary Magdalene's wonderful encounter with the Risen Lord in the Garden: 'Mary'. A photograph taken by me of the Chapel of the Ascension at the Summit of the Mount of Olives completes the first phase of the Pilgrimage, the period of our Lord's life and ministry on earth.

Berthe kindly agreed to loan me the original of 'The Living Christ' for the Pilgrimage. Weighing over 80lbs and projecting half an inch in front of the frame, transport was a problem and Berthe and Mauricette insisted on travelling with the picture in the back of the van. They supervised the unloading and accompanied their masterpiece step by step to the spot where it was to be displayed at the foot of the Upper Staircase. It was good of Berthe to loan 'The Living Christ', which she rightly regarded as her most important work.

'The Living Christ' starts us on a new era – our own era of the Crucified, Risen and Ascended Christ. This is the commencement of our Upper Staircase, a very significant part of the Pilgrimage. Berthe's original picture was returned to her gallery at the end of Christian Heritage Year. We have had copies printed and one of these now hangs in place of the original.

Before His Ascension, Jesus told the disciples: 'I am with you always . . . to the end of time.' Berthe's 'The Living Christ' represents the loving, compassionate Christ, with us now and always, through His Holy Spirit.

After Berthe's 'The Living Christ' on the Upper Staircase are pictures of a few of the countless people whose lives have been transformed by the power of the Living Christ. First, by Helen

Perrott, Paul's conversion experience on the road to Damascus. Continuing up the Staircase we come to St Francis, on his mountain, La Verna, where he spent the night in prayer and in a vision experienced the agony of the Crucifixion and our Lord's triumph over death. During this vision Francis mystically received the stigmata, the wounds of the nails in his hands and his feet, which remained until his death. Next, St Thomas More, our connection by marriage, who described himself as: 'The King's good servant but God's first.' Thomas More represents thousands of Christian martyrs who were prepared to suffer torture, ridicule and death in the cause of Christ. Young Perpetua and her companions, thrown to the wild animals in the ring at the Coliseum in front of the 'dignitaries' of Rome. St Laurence, roasted to death on a grid iron . . . The list is endless, their suffering indescribable but it was not in vain. We revere them and their example should act as a spur to our own puny efforts.

We then come to St Bernadette and her vision of the Virgin Mary at Lourdes. Our Lady told her to dig with her hands and the waters of Lourdes then commenced their flow, from which miraculous healings have been received. I mentioned to Bishop Morris Maddocks that I needed to buy prints of Bernadette at Lourdes and also of St Francis. He replied: 'I believe someone will paint those for you.' I confess to thinking this unlikely but a few weeks later, as though in response to the Bishop's intuition, I received a letter from a Mr Douglas Cooper, informing me that he was an artist. He had never had an art lesson but God had taught Douglas to paint and he believed that God wanted this gift to be used in His service. We arranged to meet and Douglas Cooper agreed to paint the two pictures we needed and they have been much admired on the Staircase.

Climbing the Staircase, each picture brings us closer to our own times, and the next is in our century – Dorothy Kerin, miraculously healed from a long and very serious illness. She had been technically dead for a few minutes and was instantly healed, to the amazement of her family gathered round the bedside. This healing is medically attested, and books and cards are available on Dorothy Kerin. After her healing, at the age of 22, Dorothy devoted her life to Christ and in obedience to His will founded Burrswood Home of Christian Healing at Groombridge, Kent, which is still very active today.

The final picture is a photograph of Sue Coles, with her testimony:

At the age of 29 I had a malignant tumour removed from my colon. Four years later I gave birth to a third daughter, and very soon afterwards I was found to have another growth and following major surgery were months of radiotherapy and chemotherapy. Then my life was shattered: another growth had shown up on an X-ray. I had faith in God and I prayed and my church prayed too. My dearest friend, Krystyna, an unbeliever, watched, comforted and helped but what could she do to heal me? She had to turn to the Lord and pray. I was taken to an Anglican healing service in Hounslow. That evening I knew I had been healed – I heard a heavenly choir singing and Jesus became very real. The day of the appointment with the consultant came - the lump had disappeared. Thank you Lord for healing me.

Krystyna was probably not the only person to become a dedicated Christian as a result of Sue's healing.

Finally, at the head of the stairwell is a full-sized cross in 350-year-old oak made by the Estate maintenance foreman, Mr Larry Sheppard: a reminder that the important healing is the final one, the healing to eternal life. St Paul reminds us: 'The gift of God is eternal life through Jesus Christ our Lord' (Rom. 6:23). It is an important reminder, particularly for those who are very ill.

At the top of the stairs is a small room which for years was a junk room; right at the top of the House, it was too remote to be used. What more appropriate at the end of a Pilgrimage than a chapel? I prayed about the details and felt led to find a carpet in light blue, regarded as the colour appropriate for healing, then a pew front surplus to requirements in our church at Littleton fitted perfectly without alteration, and the table which now forms the altar was formerly covered with junk in the passage. The clear glass window gives a view of the Creation: the fields and woods. The Dove of the Holy Spirit is etched in the top of the window. The Chapel is used at least twice daily for private prayer and the Eucharist is normally celebrated at least twice each month. It is a place of deep peace.

We have a twenty-minute professional video produced on the Staircase Pilgrimage, including three live testimonies of Christian healing, by Sue Coles, Marion Ashe and Viola Kirke, and another video on our Christian Cancer Help Centre. Both are presented by the lovely Pam Rhodes who we first met when she interviewed us on a *Songs of Praise* programme.

When the house is open to the public, the video is shown and information given on the pictures, the Christian healing ministry and the Loseley Christian Cancer Help Centre. Visitors may also spend time in the Chapel and many who are sick, bereaved or troubled have been blessed and have found there the peace of God.

The Chapel was dedicated on 9th September 1986 at a Eucharist at which Bishop Morris presided, assisted by the Reverend Pat Ashe and attended by Anne Maddocks, Marion Ashe, Mike and Sarah, and Sue and I. It was a simple and very meaningful service. The following prayers were included:

That all who enter here may be conscious of the presence of the Lord Jesus.

Having found your forgiveness, your love and your peace, may we and all those who pray here find your healing of Spirit, Mind and Body; that they may be whole to serve you. Amen.

CHAPTER 16

LOSELEY CHRISTIAN CANCER HELP CENTRE

Love, compassion and faith are essentials in Christian ministry; and for cancer sufferers, who are facing pain and death, faith is supremely important. There are many cancer self-help groups, but few Christian groups. We have some experience of non-Christian groups; the supporters are kind, helpful and encouraging and there is good advice about diet, relaxation and peace, but these groups lack the spiritual depth of a Christian group and they do not face up to the fact of death, which for the Christian means passing through to eternal life. A self-help group wrote asking if Loseley could provide two healers for one of their meetings. I telephoned the organiser explaining that we do not have any 'healers' – God heals and we are merely the channels. 'Two of us would be happy to come and pray and lay hands on your patients.' That was not what they wanted: 'Oh no, they'll think they are dying if you start praying!' We heard no further from them and the sad fact is that to most people, even when very ill, the word 'Christian' is a turn-off. We must play our part in bringing awareness of the peace and love of Christ to all. Nothing is more worthwhile.

Attitude to death is very important: two contrasting experiences are contained in my abbreviated note of 7th December 1983.

Before going to sleep one Sunday night, I read a moving passage from George Bennett's book *The Heart of Healing*. After ministering to a young nurse, too ill with cancer to walk to the sanctuary, the Revd George Bennett had visited her in her flat. She said: 'This is the first time I have been on the receiving end of prayer and it is wonderful. I've joined in prayer with my friends for the healing of many people and I am now finding what it is like to be so blessed. I know you won't feel sorry for me because paradise seems so close and I would not have this realisation taken from me for anything that anyone could give. If only we could experience a thing like this when life is normal! What a difference it would make to the world!'

By coincidence, the morning after reading of this nurse's attitude to death, Fred Gooch handed me a letter from the wife of one of our American business friends: 'This has been a heartbreaking year for us. About fifteen months ago we found out that John's daughter, Karen, had cancer of the stomach and lungs. Three months ago she moved in with us and I took a leave of absence to care for her. She is terrified of hospitals and we decided we could handle it here at home. It's an emotionally draining experience for all of us. Karen wants a lot of people round her all the time – she sleeps sitting up in the living room, she is terrified of the dark, of being alone and of a quiet house. So we keep the lights and television on twenty-four hours, the house full of company and when she is alone and afraid, I sit with her.' I wrote to Karen's family, mentioning the Christian healing ministry and my faith. I gave assurance of my prayers and offered to fly over and talk to Karen, a bright girl in her early 20s, who I had met on a business visit to the USA. The appreciative reply did not accept the offered visit.

I am sure that there could not be more human love and caring than Karen is receiving. Yet, the contrast between the nurse and Karen could hardly be more striking, both suffering from advanced stages of cancer: one filled with joy and the peace and love of God and the other filled with terror and fear of being alone.

In hospitals and homes throughout the world there are many people suffering without the knowledge of our Lord's transforming love and power. The peace of mind and freedom from fear enjoyed by a believer is a gift beyond price, and it remains on offer.

At the 1986 Acorn Christian Healing Trust Conference, Bishop Morris Maddocks, Director and co-founder of Acorn with his wife Anne, asked us all to think and pray about starting our own initiatives in our dioceses. Before the Conference was over, Dr Chris Jagger, a very active local doctor and dedicated Christian then in his 30s, with whom I am paired in the Acorn Apostolate, said to me: 'I think we should do something at Loseley, using the peace, the beauty and the organic food.' After our return home, Chris and his wife Maggie came over to Loseley to look round and we prayed together. The moat border with its peace and beauty we agreed would be an asset; the Staircase Pilgrimage and the Chapel would be important too.

After looking round the House, Gardens and Stable Yard, we drove to our hamlet of Littleton and entered the Estate church of St Francis, where a monthly Eucharist is held, led by the Revd Pat Ashe, a retired priest: a gentle, compassionate man with a wonderful record of missionary enterprise and pastoral care. With his wife Marion, Pat was already well known to Chris and Maggie.

Driving back along the lane towards Loseley we suddenly spotted, flying high above us, a large and perfect V formation of birds. We could not make out what they were: not Canada geese, which are often seen in flight in this area, but it was a sight that we found very moving and felt must be significant. The only clue was that the V pointed roughly towards the church.

The final decision was that we should offer Christian ministry to cancer patients. Both Chris and I were certain that this was right and I had felt led to minister to cancer patients for the past ten years. There was still a major problem: where were we going to house the patients?

With the sale of Guildway two years earlier, a great weight of work and responsiblity was lifted off me. Now, with Mike progressively taking over my responsibilities at Loseley, I was becoming available to spend much more time on the Lord's work. This is what I had longed to do for many years and now I was being called to minister to cancer sufferers, and a Christian Cancer Centre at Loseley of some kind would be a wonderful project to undertake. We were on the threshold of something important in which I could channel my energies to God's service. We were praying for guidance on the project and particularly about accommodation.

Early in January comes the Oxford Farming Conference; for many years an important annual event in our diaries. On this particular occasion, on 6th January 1987, I was due to take Mike and our organic farming partner, Guy Lee, leaving home at 6.45am. I went to the Chapel at about 6.30am and as soon as I knelt I had a strong feeling that I must not go to Oxford and that I should later find out what I was to do instead. Quite a test of faith. When I went down Mike was at the door, with Sue ready to see us off. 'Come on father . . .' I cut Mike short: 'I'm sorry Mike, I'm not coming. You'll have to go on with Guy. I can't explain now.'

Understandably, Sue looked worried and Mike and Guy went off to Oxford. Over breakfast I explained to Sue and then returned to the Chapel to pray for instructions. It came to me that I should go to Whitehill Chase, Bordon, which had recently become the Acorn Christian Healing Trust's Resource Centre. I went there and saw the Revd Dr Roy Walford, the warden, and outlined our ideas for using Loseley to help cancer patients. I explained that our big problem was having no residential accommodation: we were open to the public and the bedrooms in the main wing had panelling and tapestry on the walls, were very cold, with no heating or plumbing. The remainder of the House was already occupied by the eight members of the family, so there were no bedrooms available. 'You don't need bedrooms,' was Roy's unexpected and exciting response: 'I've been thinking about starting a cancer day centre here. We would welcome the patients with a cup of coffee, let them stroll in the grounds, then the Eucharist in the Chapel, light lunch followed by sharing and counselling. You could do all that at Loseley.' And we did!

In going to the Acorn Resource Centre instead of to Oxford, I had been obedient to what I believed to be God's will and now the accommodation problem was solved – we didn't need it! Next we had a get-together in the Oak Room at Loseley, Bishop Morris and Anne Maddocks, Chris Jagger, Sue and myself. After prayer, we discussed and agreed to proceed as suggested by Roy. We approved the name: The Loseley Christian Cancer Help Centre (LCCHC) associated with Acorn Christian Healing Trust. We were privileged to be the first of many Acorn-based initiatives.

The inaugural service was held on Tuesday 3rd June 1987 in the Loseley Drawing Room, led, appropriately, by the Revd Dr Roy Walford of Acorn. Forty-seven people were present, including one cancer patient and Sister Nuala FMDM, Mrs Mairi Oppenheimer, Mrs Peggy de Pemberton, Chris Jagger, Sue and myself. From that day onwards we have had two meetings of the group each month, on the first and third Tuesdays: and only once, when the weather was appalling, have we not had a cancer patient. Total numbers now are usually around thirty: we have been as low as sixteen and up to forty-four, with between seven and fourteen cancer patients at a time, the remainder being support group and spouses and friends of the patients: the need of support for the carers is as great as for the patients. Patients come from as far away as the Sussex and Hampshire coast, London, Redhill and sometimes beyond. This emphasises the great need for more of these Centres.

The LCCHC does not consist just of meetings on the first and third Tuesdays. All our patients are entered in the Intercessions Book in the Chapel and regularly remembered in prayer. Sue and I are among those who visit patients in hospital and at home if they are not well enough to come to us. We are happy also to visit and to pray with cancer patients who are diffident about coming to our meetings and those unable to come to us. We sometimes have requests for prayer for overseas patients. I know of cases of illness being healed through distant prayer – sometimes the person being healed is not previously aware of being prayed for.

The first question people often ask about the Christian Cancer Centre is: 'What happens?' The proceedings are set out on our leaflet as follows:

Any cancer sufferers and their carers are very welcome – of any denomination or none. the ministry they will receive is Christian – God's love and our love as His channels. The atmosphere is informal, warm and caring.

We meet on the first and third Tuesdays of each month. The programme is as follows:

12.30pm – Optional Eucharist in Chapel followed by ministry for any desiring it at this stage (some may then wish to go home). Please arrive at 12.20pm if attending the Eucharist.
1.15pm – Lunch. Please bring sandwiches, and we will provide ice cream, yoghourt and coffee.
2.00pm – Welcome, hymns, prayer/reading/silence.
2.45pm – Prayer and laying-on of hands for those who were unable to be present in the Chapel earlier.
3.00pm – Sharing of information.
3.45pm – Depart.

Please note that on the third Tuesday in January, April, July and October the Eucharist is at 2.00pm, not the usual 12.30pm.

Listing the programme does not give the full answer to: 'What happens?' We have always been blessed at our meetings with a wonderful atmosphere of peace, love and warmth. As we say at the beginning of the Eucharist:

> The Lord is here.
> His spirit is with us.

Peace and love, stillness and awareness of the presence of God: these are always salient features, priceless gifts, at our gatherings. I have a journal entry dated November 1988, which could have applied to any of our meetings:

> Jo W. said afterwards: 'It is the spiritual depth that makes LCCHC so special.' They all seem to feel the peace of God, the love, the openness and they respond. We in the support group are inspired by the courage and cheerfulness of the patients like Janique, who came from the hospice, so weak, to be with us yesterday. Aware of God and His peace, His love and His presence, we place ourselves unreservedly in His hands . . . through prayer and openness to His will.

We are most fortunate in having the Revd Pat Ashe, who also conducts our services at St Francis, Littleton, as Chaplain to the Christian Cancer Centre. He conducts the Eucharist and leads the prayers and laying-on of hands, which takes place during the Eucharist in the Chapel. Dr Chris Jagger plays a vital part; as well as being a very competent GP, he is an active and talented evangelical Christian, a trustee of Lee Abbey. Chris is also an accomplished musician and leads our sessions of singing with his guitar. Sue participates as well as looking after the hospitality and the comings and goings. There are no charges and no one is paid, except for one part-time helper, Melody, who has sixteen years' nursing experience, and who ensures that we keep in touch with patients by telephone and visits, in addition to helping on the group Tuesdays. During the summer months, when the House is open, Melody also staffs the Blue Room (blue is the healing colour!) and shows the videos on four afternoons a week. The dozen or so members of the support group meet quarterly to review progress and to discuss possible improvements and additional facilities.

It is not difficult to be aware of God in the Chapel, which is always blessed with a deep peace. We are aware of this peace at the Eucharist, Pat officiating, soft-voiced, full of reverence. At the end of the Eucharist and prayer for healing with laying-on of hands for the patients, we go down to the Great Hall for our picnic lunch. Of course, there is more to this than just eating; it is a relaxed time of moving round the patients, catching up on progress, consoling over setbacks, greeting first-timers, seeking news of others not here today. We are all concerned about those who have had a bad prognosis or are due to have an operation and relevant dates are carefully noted.

We are like a large family, sharing the pain, rejoicing in the good news. Sometimes a patient, who last time was looking ill and pale, arrives smiling, moving normally, so much better, and we all rejoice. We have shocks and disappointments too, like Marylynn, a lovely young wife and mother. Marylynn had had a number of ups and downs but last time she came looking so much better; now, a month later, as she entered tears came to my eyes, for she was yellow, the sign that the cancer had got to the liver and she was obviously in pain: she died a few weeks later.

I have asserted that for the Christian death is just the passing to eternal life and this awareness can remove the fear but not the sorrow. Jesus found the sisters of Lazarus weeping. Far from reprimanding them for their tears, He brought Lazarus back from the dead. He understands and has compassion for our sorrows and we take our grief to Him in prayer.

Annette came with her husband, Keith, after seeing us on the *Songs of Praise* programme in 1990. She had had breast cancer five years earlier and had been pronounced terminally ill when she first came to us, the cancer having spread to her duodenum and liver, which was inoperable. A few years later, in 1991, Annette gave her testimony on the video we were making with Pam Rhodes. She told how she had received the Holy Spirit when she had the laying-on of hands at Loseley and soon afterwards Annette was found to be clear. The specialist said: 'You're fine. What's your secret?' Pam, the interviewer, asked: 'And were you healed?' Annette, shyly smiling, said she believed that she had been healed. Some two years later Annette suffered severe abdominal pains, there were problems with liquid which had to be drained off in hospital. All was not well. We mourned deeply the death of Annette, specially remembering her in our prayers and Keith, her devoted husband, and family.

Understandably many people ask: 'Are they healed?' The world judges success by physical results and regards death as the end. In this context the answer must be: 'Many are not physically healed.' As Christians we believe that death is the final healing and we commit the dying into the hands of God. We have had remissions granted for up to four years to patients who came with three or four months life expectancy. There are clearly discernible benefits in most of our patients – emotional healings, fears turned to peace, worries drowned in a sea of love.

Andrew was a Churchwarden, aged about 70, retired from his own business and recently widowed. He first came to us the day after the 1987 windblow; the electricity supply was still off and none of us felt at our best, but Andrew was about the most dejected human being we had ever seen. He had serious lung cancer. Because of all the trees blocking the roads, there were only a few of us present at that meeting and Andrew was so depressed that there was an atmosphere of gloom that we had never experienced before or since. The second time he came Andrew was a little brighter. He brought with him his own support group of three, including Colonel Jack Wykes, now over 90, and Les Swann, who are still members of the group, both from Andrew's church at Clandon. The third time Andrew was a different person and from then on he was cheerful and uncomplaining despite his horrid coughing bouts, and a wonderful example to us all. He had a remission for over a year and when Andrew realised the end was near he turned to me and said, as casually as if he were inviting me to tea: 'I'd be awfully grateful if you would read the lesson at my funeral.' He died a week later and I fulfilled his request.

Among our early members were Tony and Anne, a lovely couple, sensitive and kind. Tony had been senior partner in his family law firm but had to retire before he was 50 due to his cancer. Tony was healed of two cancers and he seemed to be well again. There was also a need for 'inner healing' for emotional problems and this healing was also received, but then very sadly Tony developed a double brain tumour which was inoperable and he died. Years later his widow, Anne, remarried, the bridegroom being the widower of Maureen, another of our lovely patients.

All members who are very ill as well as the recently bereaved are remembered daily in prayer in the Chapel and they are never far from our thoughts. Names of wonderful, courageous people come flooding into my mind, including Jenny and her husband Roy. A year ago Jenny was unable to see the Christmas tree, she had gone blind and with the cancer spreading she thought it would be her last Christmas. This Christmas we have been giving special thanks to God, for Jenny could see the tree and her other cancers have abated.

One could tell of the courage and faith of so many . . . Vera, interviewed on video a week before she died, testifying to the great peace which she had received: 'I can relax now. I couldn't before.' And Mildred: '. . . but nothing with the Lord is "terminal". His love is eternal. We don't know about tomorrow but we know that He is in tomorrow. There is nothing to fear. Praise His name!'

Kit, the indomitable Irish lady, who came over to England as a girl into domestic service at a very low wage. Now, living alone with Ben, her ancient Labrador, Kit was riddled with pain, rheumatism, cancer, diabetes: she had the lot, yet she was always cheerful, a devout Catholic, always giving thanks to God, giving gifts to all who visited her.

Lawrie, a cancer patient, became known to a wider circle through his circulated letters full of faith, peace and hope, and with his wife Dawn was a great encouragement to the group. 'Praise the Lord' is often heard at Loseley, never: 'Why does it have to happen to me?' We remember Alf and Hazel, their courage and cheerfulness, Douglas and Valerie, Douglas and Dorothy, Juliet, looking so weak and ill but never complaining, with her staunch supporters Didi and Audrey. 11-year-old Sarah, determined to come again, even though too weak to walk from room to room, and Christine who arrived on her last visit to Loseley by ambulance on a stretcher; knowing that she had not long to live, she insisted on taking the family to Disneyland, Florida, and died at peace soon after her return.

Bill and Judy: it is difficult to remember that Commander Bill Charters is a patient, he is always so involved in supporting others. We will always remember the cheerful courage of Father Richard Veasey at Loseley during his final weeks with cancer. Father Peter from the Chilworth Franciscan Friary was another inspiring example: suffering long and painfully, including the loss of an eye through cancer, he never complained. It was only after he died that we learned that Father Peter had been a popular cabaret singer at Le Lido in the Champs Elysées, Paris! All our members are special and all deserve to be mentioned but now we must continue with the programme.

After lunch we move into the Drawing Room, sitting on green plastic armchairs with seat-pads, specially chosen by Sue for comfort, compatibility with the Drawing Room and stackability. Sometimes we have more than forty people, chairs must be easily manoeuvrable. At the start I welcome everyone, especially newcomers, giving out information on any special developments, passing on greetings from patients unable to be with us. Melody then briefly reports on her contacts, visits and messages received. Then over to Dr Chris who starts us off with Christian songs, accompanying with his guitar. Chris, now in his early 40s has many talents. With his prayer, music and praise, he increases in us awareness of the presence of God. After three or four songs, follows a relaxation of body, perhaps a short meditation. 'Let us be open to the healing love of Christ . . .' There follows a short Bible study, then prayer with laying-on of hands for those not present for this ministry at the Eucharist before lunch.

Next comes the sharing by the patients, telling us how they are, what progress has been made, or sometimes what setbacks, since our last meeting, and the results of scans and check-ups. Nearly all the patients are completely open: it is not easy to talk of these things in front of forty people but they know that we are all supportive and understanding. In the support group we also have the Revd Geoffrey Carr, a retired priest I first met when we were both visiting the cancer wards at St Luke's Hospital, Guildford, and the Revd Professor Edward Williams, a non-stipendiary minister who is also a professor in medicine.

In 1993 we had our first annual day of thanksgiving, remembrance and reunion. Timings were similar to our fortnightly meetings but the afternoon session consisted of five talks, four by bereaved members and one by Sister Nuala FMDM, who has been a valued support group member from the very first meeting, as has Mairi Oppenheimer, who also gave a talk. Mairi, widow of Simon, my last Managing Director at Guildway and finally Transport Director of Loseley Dairy Products, is a part-time receptionist at the St Luke's Hospital Cancer Centre where she is able to help patients who, understandably, often arrive full of worry and apprehension.

In my invitation to bereaved members I wrote: 'We feel very much a community – sharing in love and faith, not only with those present but also with those unable to attend, especially those in hospital and those who have passed on. We still feel linked to you and to them and even if you are unable to be with us on reunion day, you will be remembered.'

We have for years been trying to encourage the formation of other Christian cancer help centres: there is such a need for them. There are now centres at Nutbourne near Havant, Hants, Hartley Wintney and Pyrford and interest is now being shown in several other areas. It is worth repeating that there is a vast difference between a self-help cancer group and a Christian cancer group. We always emphasise that it is not necessary to be a Christian to be a patient in our group, but the ministry given is Christian, our love and compassion and ourselves as channels for God's healing love.

A ministry to which I feel specially called is praying with the very ill and the dying and this is one occasion when I prefer to work on my own with only members of the patient's family present. One is communicating with God and aware of the sick person, acting as a channel between the two. If a colleague is present, and also praying aloud, I then need to concentrate on what they are saying and this interrupts spiritual harmony. Nearly always when with someone close to death, I am aware of the presence of God and I believe that the patient shares this awareness. In awareness of that presence, one is guided to pray and I invite the family round the bedside to join in when I feel that laying-on of hands is appropriate. It is a time of great peace and only love can penetrate the barrier of sorrow, pain and fear, and especially God's love.

Just after my experience at Bronwen Astor's prayer group many years ago, I had three vivid and significant dreams, on successive nights. In one dream I was praying and there was a wonderful atmosphere of peace and love. In another dream many people were arriving at Loseley, including parties of children, for some form of Christian ministry in which I was involved. In the third and much the most powerful dream I was dying. This was the best dream I have ever experienced, such awareness of the peace and the love of God. At the time I thought of this just as being very comforting; only now do I realise that it was an important gift for this ministry. This is the very peace and love of which I am aware when praying with the dying. God is always at work. Too often we are unaware of Him.

Most years we have had a special meeting of the group to which members of the Guildford Self-Help Cancer Group are invited. After the date for one of these gatherings had been fixed, Sue and I received an invitation to the Buckingham Palace Garden Party but felt we must decline. Shortly afterwards I was asked by the Lord Lieutenant to represent him in welcoming Prince Charles at a function in the county. I explained that unfortunately I had had to decline an invitation to HM's Garden Party on that day because of our cancer group meeting and regretted that I must also decline this honour.

The day of the cancer group special meeting dawned and less than an hour before lunch the telephone rang and I was asked if I would take Francis and Judith MacNutt and their children to see the Farm animals that afternoon. Francis MacNutt is very well known in the healing ministry, an American Catholic, previously a Dominican monk and author of many books on the healing ministry. With their team from the USA, the MacNutts had just completed a three-day healing seminar at the Guildford Millmead Centre. Without hesitation I agreed to the visit and asked that the family should come to the car park at 2.30pm. It was a warm, sunny day and I arranged for the sharing session to take place seated on the lawn, in full view of the car park.

I welcomed the MacNutt family and Ruth Thornton who had brought them. I explained that the cancer patients were assembled on the lawn and I would be grateful if Francis would kindly say a few words to them. He graciously gave them over ten minutes, then his wife Judith followed and gave her testimony of healing, which she had not even mentioned at the big Guildford conference. Whereas if we had accepted the Royal Garden Party invitation the MacNutts would not have come to Loseley and we should all have missed this inspiring visit.

Judith, in her early 20s, had been diagnosed as suffering from cancer in her womb and she was informed that a hysterectomy was imperative. She declined, stating that she wished to have children and that she believed that God would heal her. A short time afterwards she received the laying-on of hands from a monk, Father MacNutt. She felt tremendous heat and believed she had been healed. The healing was confirmed by the medics and there were no more problems. There were, however, other problems, for she and the monk had fallen in love. Eventually Francis MacNutt withdrew from his Order, he and Judith married and here they were with their two splendid children. Miracles do happen. Although no longer a monk, Francis MacNutt's healing ministry continues even more strongly throughout the world.

Of the cancer group we often say: 'This is the real world', the world of suffering, but suffering in awareness of God's love and the caring love of all the members, compassion and mutual support. Away from the rat-race, competitive turmoil, the thrusting to get ahead, selfishness, the constant striving for more. This is the real world, awareness of the peace of God and caring for others.

I mentioned earlier that I regard the formation of the Loseley Co-Partnership Scheme as the most worthwhile initiative in my farming career. LCCHC, stemming from Acorn, I regard as far more worthwhile and Sue and I are not alone in feeling very privileged to be involved in it. Thanks be to God.

CHAPTER 17

EPILOGUE

I should not end without taking you on a quick tour of the House and we'll concentrate on family pictures and share a few thoughts. We enter the Great Hall from the front entrance, then up the stairs to the Minstrels' Gallery. The Hall ceiling is 20ft high and in the Gallery we are level with the portraits of my ancestors and I feel closer to them as we and they look down on the great room below. Looking straight ahead, the enormous 1739 family group is of Sir More Molyneux, his wife Cassandra and eight of their children – including Thomas, the extravagant; and Jane who, thankfully, watched the pennies.

Not much is recorded about the wives: poor things, few lived as long as their husbands. They spent a large proportion of their married lives in pregnancy, and childbirth was always dangerous, taking Anne Donne at the age of 33. When they were well, the wives organised the domestic staff, and saw to the housekeeping as well as being involved in entertaining the many visitors.

Included on the north wall are portraits of my father, the General, in uniform, and my mother's father, the Admiral, also in uniform. On our left is the portrait of my mother and on the right her uncle William M-M, on whose death my mother inherited. On the south wall to our left are other family portraits, including the full-length picture of my lovely great grandmother holding her young son Tom. Before leaving the Gallery I point out the double-glazing sashes on all those great windows, produced and fixed by Guildway for the downstairs rooms: what a difference they made to our comfort!

We return down the stairs and go across the Great Hall, marvelling at the perspective in the panelling at the end of the room, originally produced for Henry VIII's Nonsuch Palace. The next room is the Library, cosy, a fraction of the size of the Great Hall, its ceiling only 10ft high, and walls lined with bookcases.

There are no hanging portraits, but on the table in the corner we come into our own era, with photographs. Sue, Mike and I at the Palace with my OBE in 1983. Next, in 1984, HRH the Duke of Kent presenting me with the RASE Bledisloe Gold Medal for Landowners. This award had been made only fifteen times in the past twenty-five years. I could never have dreamed of this, a gold medal, not in 1984, let alone 1947!

The next photograph (included in the illustrations), is far more important than medals; Mike and Sarah's four children. Whatever Mike and Sarah may achieve in the future, they could not do anything better for Loseley than produce those four splendid children. For the past hundred years, three generations produced only three children between us. Mike is a much better father than I was and, with Loseley now in better condition, he and Sarah in their situation can have different priorities from Sue and I when we took over. The children were recently on Danish television; Alexander, the eldest, hitting the bull's eye with his archery; elegant and accomplished Katrina, ballet dancer, ice skater, with her cups and trophies; Christopher, like Alexander an excellent skier, was playing the drums and tying fishing flies; Tristram, the youngest, being his happy self.

Before leaving the Library, we notice the picture above the door of the House with Sir George's wing containing the Chapel, pulled down in 1820. When HRH Princess Margaret saw the picture, she asked: 'Do you have a Chapel now?' I had to admit that sadly we did not. I had long been pondering about a Chapel and this was the spur that I needed.

We move on to the Drawing Room; it is here that the afternoon session of the Christian Cancer Group takes place. Now we sit and take in the elegance and peace of this room, the great carved chalk chimneypiece, the gilded ceiling decorated for the visit of James I and his Queen, the chairs and cabinets that Paul Getty had coveted. Facing us, left of the fireplace, is a portrait of the builder, Sir William More, with flowing white beard, wearing a ruff and a thoughtful, solemn expression. How did he manage to get through all his duties? Surely the greatest of all the owners of Loseley, though not a greater man than St Thomas More, whose portrait hangs on the other side.

Sir William's son, Sir George More, with flushed cheeks, neat little beard and moustache, fair to auburn in colour. 'Little but good', though John Donne may have had reservations. Next, owner at the time of the Civil War, Sir Poynings More Bt, in armour, dark hair, beard and moustache; coarser, thicker-lipped than his predecessors, but handsome.

The full-length portrait of my beautiful great-grandmother Caroline complements the grace and beauty of this Drawing Room. The Revd Nicholas More and his son Robert, who both inherited, are among the other portraits. We leave the Drawing Room under the eyes of Anne Boleyn, the cause of Thomas More's execution; before long she herself was to follow him to the scaffold.

Turning right on leaving the Drawing Room we come to the Pilgrimage Staircase. This has been described earlier and we go up in silence, letting the pictures speak to us of the life of Jesus and the Saints. At the top stands the cross. We enter the Chapel and spend a minute or two in silent prayer, aware of deep peace: 'Be still and know that I am God.' Before leaving, we look down through the window at the Creation: the fields with cattle and sheep grazing, and woods, including a young plantation named Susan's Wood. There is light rain falling, giving a special softness to the green fields, and for a moment the sun streaks through.

Now we go along the Top Floor, restored to being the Long Gallery, after a century of accommodating servants. How cold they must have been, getting up at 5am to black-lead the grates, light the fires, remove the slops, bring up the hot water . . . but at least they had a job, food and companionship; many were worse off.

I have mentioned among her household chores, Sue's opening and closing of all the windows in the House. I sometimes volunteered to shut the windows on a summer evening; Sue knew I would take a long time at it, for I always got immersed in thought, looking out over the fields. So much to think about, such beauty in the evening light. I must try not to get too carried away.

Now I'm thinking about how this view has changed in our fifty years. Not that much. It's tidier; when I started there were fallen trees still lying on the ground and there were brambles and thorn bushes in the fields. Sadly my father at first resented the removal of brambles and thorns, for he loved nature wild and didn't take to brash efficiency, but he and I were very close and he understood my motives. The old wire fence between the lawn and the Front Park has been replaced by a post-and-rail fence 100 yards further down the field. This was one of Sue's bright ideas, to give space for more marquees and leisure events held on the lawn.

Front Park has now been organic for over twenty years, no artificial fertiliser, no chemical sprays. Sue and I long held the ambition to turn over all the Loseley land to organic, working in harmony with nature, producing food that is really healthy. For a time we had one of the dairy farms completely organic, and for seven years a 300-acre farm was all organic in a partnership with Guy and Philippa Lee. From our organic wheat we produced stone-ground flour for sale to housewives and bakers, and for the Loseley Organic Bakery. Our Walled Garden was fully organic and we expanded with a field of organic vegetables, strawberries and raspberries. We planned to increase this acreage and to start commercial processing into organic soups and frozen vegetables, building a business to rival Loseley Dairy Products. That proved an enterprise too far; we did not have a Fred Gooch or Daphne Holloway to manage the project; we then lost our organic partners, who bought a farm in Scotland. At the time when Mike took over from me no one was interested in carrying on the organic farming, it was not considered profitable: it was not Mike's fault, though, being college trained, he did not share his parents' enthusiasm for 'muck and moonshine'.

A final look through the window: to the left and beyond Front Park are the free-range pigs rootling in the soil, changing the landscape from green to brown. They had a very special and distinguished summer visitor, the Most Revd the Rt Hon. Lord Coggan no less. Unexpectedly, in that sense, the heavens opened and Donald Coggan got drenched, but he made light of it and continued to smile. He loves pigs and the pigs were glad to see him but delighted in the refreshing rain rather more than we did!

At the head of the back spiral stairs, in earlier times used only by staff, we pass the turret clock and wind our way down to the back passage. We ourselves normally use the back door rather than the front, so we'll go out that way for a quick look in the Walled Garden. No time to stroll on the terrace or down the moat border, a favourite walk between the herbaceous border and the moat with its carp and water lilies. Through the newly cut-back yew hedge to see Mike and Sarah's project in progress, the great gardener Bernie Burnip working all hours of daylight, seven days a week, transforming our organic vegetable garden to formal gardens. We've come full circle, for after the war I had to be drastic. We removed over 1,000 yards of slug-infested low box hedges, the overgrown rose garden and the rotting trellis, and 200 old fruit trees. Again, my father was not too happy, but we did bring him into discussions with the experts and we found a new home for some of his special apple trees. Now Mike and Sarah are returning the garden to landscaped formality on a grander scale than it was before my time. In 1947 we could not afford to pay wages for any job that was not productive, so had to concentrate on growing vegetables. Loseley shrugs its shoulders as each generation moulds it to their thinking, to the requirements of their time.

I must now show you to your car. I haven't any eggs in my pocket like my father but here's a pot of Loseley cream to take home.

Do I have regrets? Yes, of course, but nothing compared to awareness of how much I have to be thankful for, for the challenge and for Sue to join with me in tackling it, for the beauty of Loseley and the excitement of building and developing businesses with people but, above all, for having been led into God's service.

It would have been good for Loseley and Guildway if I had been better at making money, but I put a high value on the reputation which the two businesses built up for quality, service and straight-dealing. Profit sharing and Co-Partnership provided a sound basis for a good relationship with all who worked with us.

People do matter, and caring for people, in whatever capacity, must be right. Why is paternalism regarded in our country as a dirty word?

Pioneering a new system of house construction in the UK is a hazardous venture, some would say impossible without adequate capital. I now realise that the Guildway Challenge was often more testing than the Loseley Challenge and it took a great deal of my time and energy, underpinned by my growing faith.

At Loseley we were among the first to manufacture and market additive-free dairy products on the Farm and for years we have been among the few who believed in organic farming and in wholeness. I still believe in these things. The health of the soil and of our livestock is fundamentally important, not least for human health and wellbeing.

The Christian healing ministry is certainly not new. Our Lord instructed His disciples: 'Heal the sick.' They obeyed and so must we. It is exciting to be involved, in a small way and to witness the revival of this important ministry: as exciting as building up a business and even more rewarding!

It is said that 'to travel hopefully is better than to arrive' and Sue and I have been richly blessed on our stage of the journey.

The Loseley Challenge continues, as Sue and I complete handing over our stewardship to Mike and Sarah.

Morus, the Loseley mulberry tree, survives and more have been planted.

Mike and Sarah, Alexander, Katrina, Christopher and Tristram – we wish you continuing success in meeting the Challenge and may you enjoy your time at Loseley as much as we have done.

APPENDIX

Further Reading

There are many good books on faith and the healing ministry. As a starter I would suggest *The Heart Of Healing* by George Bennett, £4.49, from Crowhurst (below). Also *A Healing House of Prayer* by Morris Maddocks (Hodder and Stoughton), £8.99. *The Christian Healing Ministry* by Morris Maddocks (SPCK) is an authoritative and comprehensive guide, available from Acorn (below), £9.99, by post £10.99. *Fear No Evil* by David Watson (Hodder and Stoughton), £3.99. *The Servant Son: Jesus Then and Now* by Donald Coggan (Triangle), £4.99.

Christian Healing Centres

The following will send details of facilities, book list and information available:

The Acorn Christian Healing Trust Resource Centre, Whitehill Chase, Bordon, Hants, GU35 OAP, (01420 472779).
Burrswood Christian Home of Healing, Groombridge, Kent, TN3 9PY, (01892 863637).
The Old Rectory, Crowhurst, near Battle, East Sussex, TN33 9AD, (01424 830204).
Harnhill Manor, near Cirencester, Gloucestershire, GL7 5PX, (01285 850283).

Christian Cancer Help Centres

Loseley, near Guildford, Surrey: contact James or Sue, (01483 66090).

Pyrford, near Woking, Surrey: contact Yvonne, (01932 347602).
Hartley Wintney, Hants: contact Angela, (01252 842247).
Weston House, Southbourne, Emsworth, Hants: contact Greta, (01243 373351).

The Loseley Videos (each twenty minutes)

Steps Of Faith including the Staircase Pilgrimage and three personal testimonies of healing, £12.50 including postage.

Christian Cancer Help giving details and personal testimonies, £12.50 including postage.

Available from Loseley Christian Trust, Loseley Park, Guildford, Surrey, GU3 1HS (how privileged we are to have that postcode!).

*   *   *

Mike More-Molyneux now runs Loseley. Changes are being made and the House is not always open. It is advisable to telephone before visiting to check on opening arrangements.

Details of the opening of Loseley House, Farm Tours and Events from Estate Office at above address, (01483 304440).